Greek Apocryphal Gospels, Fragments and Agrapha

Greek Apocryphal Gospels, Fragments and Agrapha

Introductions and Translations

Rick Brannan

LEXHAM PRESS

Greek Apocryphal Gospels, Fragments, and Agrapha: Introduction and Translations

Copyright 2017 Lexham Press

Lexham Press, 1313 Commercial St., Bellingham, WA 98225
LexhamPress.com

Print ISBN 9781683590651

Lexham Editorial Team: Rebecca Brant, Elliot Ritzema, Danielle Thevenaz
Cover Design: Brittany Schrock

For Amy, Ella, Lucas, and Josiah

Contents

Preface..ix

Introduction..1

Agrapha...7

The Protevangelium of James 35

The Infancy Gospel of Thomas..56

The Gospel of Peter 67

The Gospel of Thomas (Greek Portions) 81

The Gospel of Nicodemus (Acts of Pilate) and Descent of
    Christ into Hades 92

The Gospel of Mary (Greek Portions) 127

Fragments 134

Bibliography.. 176

— *Preface*

This is a book that almost didn't happen. Actually, it is a book that wasn't planned. As I was working on Greek editions of this material for a different project, I had no plans to translate the material, only to write intro ductions. But in the process of writing the introductions to the agrapha and fragments, I ended up translating the material anyway. So I decided to finish what I'd started and translate the rest.

For the longer material, it made sense to begin with existing translations and modernize them, in consultation with the underlying editions. So *Protevangelium of James*, *Infancy Gospel of Thomas*, and *The Gospel of Nicodemus (Acts of Pilate)* and *Descent of Christ to Hades* all have their genesis with M.R. James' edition of the New Testament Apocrypha. As I reviewed the translation, I consulted Tischedorf's edition of the Greek and made changes as I saw fit. For *The Gospel of Peter* (P.Cair. 10759), I used H.B. Swete's edition as a starting point and consulted his edition of the Greek.

For the fragmentary material, two types of translation are provided. One which I call a "reading translation," which has the material as a paragraph, intended to be read as a whole unit. The other translation, a "line translation," keeps each line as representing the transcribed line, complete with brackets indicating supplied material.

Select bibliographies of material are included at the end of each section. A larger, more inclusive bibliography can be found at the end of this volume.

I am grateful to Elliot Ritzema and Rebecca Brant for their work in copyediting this material. Their effort has sharpened my original writing and truly made it better. Any shortcomings, of course, remain my own.

It is my hope that this material will not only familiarize the reader with some of the noncanonical material floating around in the early days of the church, but will also help the reader to see the different ways the early church struggled with and tried to understand some of the more difficult notions of Christianity. Not only that, but seeing how early Christians appealed to sayings of Jesus (genuine or not) will help one understand how these people understood who Jesus was, what he did, and how it all affected their lives. It is almost like peeking in on a centuries-old conversation, just to see what we can learn.

Rick Brannan
January, 2013

Then the King of glory took hold of the head of the chief ruler Satan, and delivered him to the angels and said, "Bind down his hands and his feet and his neck and his mouth with irons." And then he delivered him to Hades, saying, "Take him and keep him safely until my second coming."—Descent of Christ to Hades 6 (22).2

— *Introduction*

The apocryphal gospels, fragments and agrapha (henceforth simply "apocryphal gospels") are important primary source materials that document the beliefs of the early church. Written after the ministry of Christ and the apostles, this collection of writings is not considered to be divinely inspired. Nevertheless, the apocryphal gospels are useful in tracing the history of the early church and its understanding of the teachings of Christ and his apostles.

Unfortunately, apocryphal gospels can also be sensational. They report fantastic things that often contradict or call into question the canonical Gospels. Their sensational nature makes them attractive to use for tasks that they really should not be used for, such as supporting particular viewpoints in the debates about the historical Jesus. Regarding their proper use, Meier notes:

> These apocryphal gospels are very important, but they belong in a study of the patristic Church from the 2nd to the 4th century. Unfortunately, the public and the press, not to mention publishers and universities, are much more interested in sensational studies about the NT than in "dull" studies of the patristic Church. In recent years we have been witnessing the "selling" of the apocrypha to these audiences under the guise of NT research and the quest for the historical Jesus. This is a misuse of useful material. There is nothing here that can serve as a source in our quest for the historical Jesus.

> To use these texts on what is from the start a precarious venture would render the venture completely incredible.[a]

Meier rightly places the material in the context of the second through fourth centuries and beyond. Thus the apocryphal gospels say less about Jesus in the context of the first century and more about the problems and issues people in later centuries had in understanding Jesus, and how they tried to solve those problems.

These early Christians were not unique. People today have similar issues and problems. As the writer of Ecclesiastes declares, "there is nothing new under the sun" (Eccl 1:9–11). Through understanding the approaches taken by early Christians, perhaps we can learn more about how we might deal with difficult issues.

For instance, the *Protevangelium of James* (*Prot. Jas.*) is an apocryphal gospel that provides a back-story for Mary and Joseph, embellishing it with details of Jesus' birth unavailable in the canonical Gospels. Instead of either throwing it away as unhelpful for understanding the historical Jesus, or going to the other extreme of preferring it to the canonical Gospels, it should be viewed as an attempt by the early church to grapple with the notion of the virgin birth. These people understood basic human physiology and reproduction, and they saw the impossibility of a virgin becoming pregnant and giving birth as much as we do. *Prot. Jas.* is a way of dealing with that difficulty, almost in the same way that the *Left Behind* series was a way of trying to explain a particular eschatological perspective.

GOSPELS, FRAGMENTS, AND AGRAPHA

The title of this book mentions "Apocryphal Gospels, Fragments, and Agrapha." These are separate classes of things typically included in treatments of "apocryphal gospels." Brief descriptions, along with listings of included material, are provided below. Detailed descriptions and introductions to the fragments and agrapha are provided in the appropriate sections of this book.

---

a. John P. Meier, "Sources: The Agrapha and the Apocryphal Gospels," in *A Marginal Jew: Rethinking the Historical Jesus*, vol. 1, *The Roots of the Problem and the Person*, Anchor Bible Reference Library (New York: Doubleday, 1991), 1:124.

GOSPELS

The gospels are longer, typically (though not always) complete works that tell a story about Jesus' life. In this book, the gospels are divided into three different types:

- **Infancy Gospels.** These are gospels that center on the child Jesus:

    - The Protevangelium of James

    - The Infancy Gospel of Thomas

- **Passion Gospels.** These are gospels that center on Jesus' passion: his trial and resurrection:

    - The Gospel of Peter

    - The Gospel of Thomas (Greek Fragments)

    - The Gospel of Nicodemus (Acts of Pilate) and the Descent of Christ to Hades

- **Post-Resurrection Gospel.** This gospel centers on post-resurrection appearances of Jesus:

    - The Gospel of Mary (Greek Fragment)

FRAGMENTS

The term "fragments" refers to the remains of papyrus and parchment materials that have been found, particularly in Egypt. These fragments contain stories of Jesus that quote or allude to canonical material or are completely unknown. They cannot be reliably placed within a larger gospel or writing, so they are treated separately.

The following fragmentary material is included:

- Dura Parchment 24

- P.Berol. 11710

- P.Cairo 10735

- P.Egerton 2 (+ P.Köln 255)

- P.Merton 51

- P.Oxy. 210

- P.Oxy. 840

- P.Oxy. 1224

- P.Oxy. 5072

- P.Vindobonensis G. 2325 (Fayum Gospel Fragment)

Each of these has some relationship with canonical gospel material (e.g., P.Merton 51) or provides previously unknown (and many times dubious) stories of Jesus during his ministry (e.g., P.Oxy. 840).

AGRAPHA

The term "agrapha" comes from a Greek word meaning "unwritten." These are sayings attributed to Jesus that were not included in the canonical Gospels. The agrapha are useful for understanding how people talked about Jesus and how people appealed to Jesus' authority in their writings. This book compiles agrapha from the following sources:

- Sayings in the Canonical New Testament Outside of the Gospels

  - Acts 20:35

  - 1 Cor 7:10–11

  - 1 Cor 9:14

  - 1 Cor 11:23–25

  - 2 Cor 12:8–9

  - 1 Thess 4:15–17

- Sayings in Additions to New Testament Manuscripts

  - Matt 20:28, Bezae

  - Mark 9:49, Bezae

- Mark 16:14, Washingtonianus (the "Freer Logion")

- Luke 6:4, Bezae

- Luke 10:16, Bezae

- John 8:7; 10–11, Bezae

• Sayings in the Apostolic Fathers

  - *Barn.* 7.11

  - *1 Clem.* 13.2

  - *2 Clem.* 3.2

  - *2 Clem.* 4.2

  - *2 Clem.* 4.5

  - *2 Clem.* 5.2–4

  - *2 Clem.* 8.5

  - *2 Clem.* 12.2–6

  - *2 Clem.* 13.2

  - *2 Clem.* 13.4

• Sayings in Justin Martyr

  - Dialogue with Trypho 35.3

  - Dialogue with Trypho 47.5

CONCLUSION

Each major section of this book offers advice for the use of apocryphal gospel material in the context of biblical studies. Each document, fragment, or saying is discussed with its relationship to canonical material in mind.

In general, this means focusing not on how the material might change our understanding of the Jesus of the New Testament, but instead on how the author/compiler of this material understood Jesus by considering how he is portrayed. It involves placing these insights not back into the world of the New Testament, but leaving them in the world of the author.

In many situations, authors are dealing with problematic areas—questions that canonical material simply does not address. Evaluating their appropriation of Jesus to address these questions gives insight into the issues themselves. Some of these are timeless questions, such as: How could a virgin give birth? What happened after Jesus died?

The apocryphal gospels do not provide authoritative answers. But they do confirm that early Christians struggled with the same things we do, and they shed light on how those Christians tried to answer these difficult (and largely unanswerable) questions. In this respect the apocryphal gospels are comforting and insightful—and a productive area of study.

— *Agrapha*

The term "agrapha" comes from the Greek word ἄγραφος (*agraphos*), which means "unwritten." In its original usage, the term indicated "unwritten" sayings of Jesus, sayings that did not occur in the four canonical Gospels.[a] Some use the term to refer strictly to extracanonical sayings considered to be authentic; others use it to refer to any sayings attributed to Jesus with no burden of authenticity.[b] It is the latter usage that will be used in this book.

SOURCES

Agrapha are typically mined from the following sources:[c]

1. Sayings in the canonical New Testament outside of the Gospels

2. Sayings in additions or variations to New Testament manuscripts

3. Sayings in earlier church fathers[d]

4. Sayings in later church fathers

5. Sayings in Islamic sources

6. Sayings in Jewish sources

7. Sayings in fragmentary nonbiblical manuscripts

---

a. W. D. Stroker, "Agrapha," *ABD* 1:92.

b. Hans-Josef Klauck, *Apocryphal Gospels: An Introduction* (London: T&T Clark, 2004), 6–7.

c. E. M. Yamauchi, "Agrapha," *ISBE* 1:69. The list is based on Yamauchi's list, but restated and expanded somewhat.

d. In this book, item 3 is further split into "Sayings in the Apostolic Fathers" and "Sayings in Justin Martyr."

8. Sayings in apocryphal gospels and acts

Items 1–3 are included in the agrapha contained in this book, but only those sources that are available in Greek. The collection includes passages thought by many to be possible sayings of Jesus,[e] but the list is not exhaustive.[f] Agrapha in items 7 and 8 are represented in the **Fragments** and **Gospels** sections of this book.[g]

USE OF AGRAPHA IN BIBLICAL STUDIES

The agrapha are important in biblical studies because they are purported sayings of Jesus. Used rightly, they help provide a picture of a particular era or region's understanding of Jesus.

The agrapha have been misunderstood, however, because they have been used to determine genuine and non-genuine sayings of Jesus. This is best seen in the area of "Historical Jesus" research. Here Craig A. Evans takes the members of the Jesus Seminar to task for their reliance on extracanonical material:

> Much controversy has been recently generated by the claim, made mostly by members of the Jesus Seminar, a North American phenomenon, that the canonical Gospels are not in fact the oldest and most reliable sources for Jesus research. Jesus Seminar members, particularly John Dominic Crossan, have argued that several extra-canonical (or apocryphal) Gospels contain traditions that predate some of the traditions preserved in the canonical Gospels. The most notable of these extra-canonicals are the *Gospel of Thomas*, the Egerton Papyrus 2, the *Gospel of Peter*, and the *Secret Gospel of Mark*. But critical study of these documents has persuaded few scholars

---

e. O. Hofius, "Isolated Sayings of the Lord," in *New Testament Apocrypha*, rev. ed., ed. Wilhelm Schneemelcher; trans. R. McL. Wilson (Louisville: Westminster John Knox, 1991), 1:88–91; M. R. James, *The Apocryphal New Testament* (Oxford: Clarendon, 1924); Bart D. Ehrman and Zlatko Pleše, *The Apocryphal Gospels: Texts and Translations* (Oxford: Oxford University Press, 2010); Klauck, *Apocryphal Gospels*.

f. For the most recent wide-ranging collection of agrapha, see William D. Stroker, *Extracanonical Sayings of Jesus* (Atlanta: Society of Biblical Literature, 1989).

g. Note, however, that no apocryphal acts are contained in this volume.

that they contain anything of genuine value. Jesus research will not make progress if it relies on these dubious sources.[h]

This quote from Evans shows how understandings of extracanonical material drive understandings of Jesus. Evans does not see such material as genuine, thus it has no place in the argument—they are "dubious sources." Crossan and others in the Jesus Seminar hold them in a higher estimation (and portions of the canonical Gospels in lower estimation)[i] and they play a much more prominent role. But the whole argument is predicated on whether certain extracanonical writings are authentic.

Focusing on this material only as a test of one's view of Jesus is too narrow. The maximal benefit of the agrapha can be gained with the following approach:

- **Analyze the saying in context.** Understand what it contributes to the immediate context. Also consider any other sayings of Jesus in the same document.

- **Consider *why* a saying of Jesus is being appealed to.** What does the authority of Jesus bring to the argument or situation?

- **Consider who is making the argument.** Where does the text come from, and what is the author's interest in making this argument?

- **Consider what this says about the author's conception of Jesus.** By considering the author's aims and goals and the sorts of things he appeals to the authority of Jesus for, a fuller picture of the author's conception of Jesus can be painted. This, in turn, can help in understanding the conception of Jesus in a particular era or geographic region.

---

h. Craig A. Evans, "The Life of Jesus," in *Handbook to the Exegesis of the New Testament*, ed. S. E. Porter, New Testament Tools and Studies 25 (Leiden: Brill, 1997), 432–33.

i. J. D. Crossan, *The Cross That Spoke: The Origins of the Passion Narrative* (San Francisco: Harper & Row, 1988); J. D. Crossan, *Four Other Gospels: Shadows on the Contours of Canon* (New York: Harper & Row, 1985).

These are sensible steps whether a saying of Jesus is found within the canon or outside of it.

SAYINGS IN THE CANONICAL NEW TESTAMENT OUTSIDE OF THE GOSPELS

Outside the canonical Gospels, New Testament writers appeal to the words of Christ with some frequency. Many of these uses are based in material found in the canonical gospels. For example, Acts 1:4 and 11:16 both likely have roots in Luke 24:49. It is difficult to distinguish from the text whether these are quotations of a saying or remembrances of something said by Jesus.

There is some consensus that the following passages are sayings of Jesus without direct roots in the canonical gospels:

- Acts 20:35

- 1 Corinthians 7:10–11

- 1 Corinthians 9:14

- 1 Corinthians 11:23–25

- 2 Corinthians 12:8–9

- 1 Thessalonians 4:15–17

Each of these will be briefly discussed below.

ACTS 20:35

The agraphon found in Acts 20:35 occurs at the end of Paul's farewell speech to the Ephesian elders (Acts 20:17–35). In the speech, Paul reminds the Ephesian elders of his time with them. He speaks of how he proclaimed the gospel to them (24), how overseers were appointed (28), how conflict will come in his absence (29–31), and how he worked to meet his own financial needs (34). Paul uses this as his basis for claiming "it is necessary to help those who are in need," which he then reiterates with a request to remember "the words of the Lord Jesus that he himself said, 'It is more blessed to give than to receive.' " Here the words of Jesus provide support and authority to Paul's request.

Parallels

In Matt 10:8, the words of Jesus include "freely you have received; freely give."

Codex Bezae (D, 05) has a slightly different version of the words of Jesus in Acts 20:35: "Blessed is the one who gives rather than the one who receives," which shifts the focus of the saying from the action (giving) to the doer (one who gives).[j]

In the Apostolic Fathers, 1 *Clem.* 2.1 mentions "giving more gladly than receiving," but does not attribute this to Jesus.

There are several passages in early Christian literature where giving is contrasted with receiving (*Did.* 1.5; 4.5; Herm. *Mand.* 2.4–5; see also *Apos. Con.* 4.2–3).[k]

Translation

I have shown you with respect to all things that by working hard in this way it is necessary to help those who are in need, and to remember the words of the Lord Jesus that he himself said, "It is more blessed to give than to receive." (Ac 20:35 LEB)

1 CORINTHIANS 7:10–11

This agraphon comes in the midst of a discussion of marriage in the first letter to the Corinthians. Paul has just commended the lifestyle of one wholly devoted to Christ (1 Cor 7:7–8) with the allowance of marriage for those who cannot contain their lust (9).

Paul next gives his thoughts on divorce. He is clear to state which portions come "from the Lord" (10–11) and which come from him (12ff). The portion attributed to "the Lord" contains the absolute commands, "... a wife must not separate from her husband.... And a husband must not divorce his wife." Paul appeals to the authority of the Lord for the basic rule, and this sets the tone of the discussion: divorce is not to be permitted.

---

j. J. A. Fitzmyer, *The Acts of the Apostles: A New Translation with Introduction and Commentary*, Anchor Bible 31 (New York: Doubleday, 1998), 682.

k. Stroker, *Extracanonical Sayings of Jesus*, 227–28.

Parallels

Mark 10:1–12 and Matt 19:1–12 reflect Jesus' teaching on divorce in the gospels. Shorter forms of this same basic teaching are found in Matt 5:31–32 and Luke 16:18. The notion of Mark 10:9, "Therefore what God has joined together, man must not separate" is reflected in Paul's appeal to the words of the Lord, but the wording is completely different.

Clement of Alexandria quotes a saying of the Lord on divorce as well: "Again the Lord says, 'Let him who is married not send (his wife) away, and let him who is not married not marry; let him who has confessed not to marry according to a resolve for sexual abstinence remain unmarried.'" (Clement, *Strom.* 3.15.97).[1] Clement aligns with Paul's attitude on the question.

Translation

To the married I command—not I, but the Lord—a wife must not separate from her husband. But if indeed she does separate, she must remain unmarried or be reconciled to her husband. And a husband must not divorce his wife. (1 Co 7:10–11 LEB)

1 Corinthians 9:14

Here Paul establishes that he has a right to make a living from his proclamation of the gospel. He appeals to the Law's description of the rights of the priests (1 Cor 9:13), perhaps as found in Num 18:8–24, making the parallel with those attending to the gospel (14). Paul will later note that while he has waived this right, it was his to waive (17–18).

Parallels

The synoptic Gospels note that the worker is worthy of his wages (Matt 10:10; Luke 10:7). The same notion is found in 1 Tim 5:18, specifically in the context of rewarding elders who serve well.

Didache 13.1–2, in an extended section about the support of prophets and teachers, notes, "But every true prophet wishing to reside among you is worthy of his food. Similarly a true teacher is himself also worthy, just

---

1. Ibid., 207.

as the worker, of his food." From here it progresses to a discussion of setting aside firstfruits for these prophets and teachers.

Translation

In the same way also the Lord ordered those who proclaim the gospel to live from the gospel. (1 Co 9:14 LEB)

1 Corinthians 11:23–25

In using this agraphon, Paul offers a corrective to the improper practice of the Lord's Supper in Corinth. The Corinthians' practice is detailed in 1 Cor 11:17–22. In verse 23, Paul begins contrasting their practice with his, which he "received from the Lord" and "passed on to you." Paul identifies problems and then appeals to the authority of the Lord in correcting those problems.

Parallels

The closest parallel to Paul's wording is found in Luke 22:19–20. The primary difference between Luke and Paul is Paul's claim to have directly received this practice from the Lord. Other canonical parallels are Matt 26:26–29 and Mark 14:22. Further, *Apostolic Constitutions and Canons* 8.12.37 covers the same material, but in different form and with additions.[m] *Didache* 9.1–5 discusses the Lord's Supper, also in a different form.

Translation

For I received from the Lord what I also passed on to you, that the Lord Jesus, on the night in which he was betrayed, took bread, and after he had given thanks, he broke it and said, "This is my body which is for you. Do this in remembrance of me." Likewise also the cup, after they had eaten, saying, "This cup is the new covenant in my blood. Do this, as often as you drink it, in remembrance of me." (1 Co 11:23–25 LEB)

2 Corinthians 12:8–9

This agraphon occurs in the context of Paul discussing his "thorn in the flesh" (2 Cor 12:7). Paul knows those who have received revelatory visions

---

m. Ibid., 174.

(1–4), and will gladly boast of those great things others have seen. Yet he will only boast of his own weaknesses (5), explaining that the "thorn in the flesh" keeps him from exalting himself (6–7). Paul appeals to the Lord for the removal of it (8), and the agraphon is the Lord's response to Paul (9). It serves as a corrective to Paul's desire for the magnificent, wonderful, revelatory things. While he desires those things, he is content that he must instead stand on the word of the Lord, that the grace of Christ is sufficient, and visions and revelations are not. Paul's response is to delight in the "weakness" of grace, being strengthened when he is tested and has nothing else upon which to stand (10).

Parallels

There are no close parallels to this agraphon.

Translation

Three times I appealed to the Lord about this, that it would depart from me. And he said to me, "My grace is sufficient for you, because the power is perfected in weakness." Therefore rather I will boast most gladly in my weaknesses, in order that the power of Christ may reside in me. (2 Co 12:8–9 LEB)

1 Thessalonians 4:15–17

This agraphon, while not including a direct quotation from the Lord, indicates the Lord as the source. In 1 Thess 4:13, Paul introduces the subject of death in Christ and the Lord's return, noting that he does not want the Thessalonian believers to be ignorant "concerning those who have fallen asleep." Paul does not simply explain; he appeals to "the word of the Lord" as providing the basis for what happens to believers who die and what will happen with them at the resurrection.

Parallels

There are no close parallels to this agraphon.

Translation

For this we say to you by the word of the Lord, that we who are alive, who remain until the Lord's coming, will not possibly precede those who have fallen asleep. For the Lord himself will descend from heaven with a shout of command, with the voice of the archangel and with the trumpet of God, and the dead in Christ will rise first. Then we who are alive, who remain, will be snatched away at the same time together with them in the clouds for a meeting with the Lord in the air, and thus we will be together with the Lord always. (1 Th 4:15–17 LEB)

SAYINGS IN ADDITIONS TO NEW TESTAMENT MANUSCRIPTS

Some manuscripts of the Greek New Testament have unique variations that record alternate versions or even completely different sayings of Jesus. Most of the sayings in this section are taken from what is known as Codex Bezae, a fifth-century document with the text of the Gospels and Acts in both Greek and Latin. It has a number of unique readings and is known for its idiosyncrasies, particularly in the book of Acts. One reading (an insertion at Mark 16:14 known as the "Freer Logion") is taken from Codex Washingtonianus, a fourth- or fifth-century document. The following variations are examined here:

- Matthew 20:28 (Bezae)

- Mark 9:49 (Bezae)

- Mark 16:14 (Washingtonianus)

- Luke 6:4 (Bezae)

- Luke 10:16 (Bezae)

- John 8:7, 10–11 (Bezae)

Each of these will be briefly discussed below. The English translation of each passage is by the author unless otherwise specified.

MATTHEW 20:28 (BEZAE)

This agraphon, which Metzger calls "a piece of floating tradition,"[n] is inserted at the end of the pericope where the mother of James and John

---

n. Bruce M. Metzger, ed., *A Textual Commentary on the Greek New Testament*, 2nd rev. ed. (New York: United Bible Societies, 1994), 43.

requests that her sons sit in an exalted place in the kingdom (Matt 20:21). After disqualifying them from such an honor (22–23) and dealing with the ruckus caused among the other disciples by the request (24–25), Jesus goes on to teach that the one who wants to be great must become a servant, following the model of the Son of Man (27–28). In this context, it is an expansion that gives the disciples specific instruction on how to serve.

Parallels

Luke 14:8–10 offers what Metzger terms "an expanded but inferior version"[o] of this material. It is also similar in conception to Jas 2:1–7.

Translation

"But you, seek to increase from what is small and to be less from what is more. And upon entering and being called in to eat, do not recline in the place of prominence, else someone more esteemed than you might come in and the one who invited you to dinner might come and say to you, 'Move down further.' and you will be shamed. But if you move back into the lower place and a person less important than you comes, the one who invited you to dinner will say, 'Come still higher' and this will be to your benefit." (Mt 20:28 Brannan)

MARK 9:49 (BEZAE)

Bezae as well as manuscripts that reflect the Old Latin tradition have "For every sacrifice will be salted with salt" instead of "For everyone will be salted with fire." Some other manuscripts, including Alexandrinus,[p] include both forms: "For everyone will be salted with fire, and every sacrifice will be salted with salt."[q]

Mark 9:42–49 is about withstanding the temptation to sin. Jesus states that it is better to lose the offending body part than to succumb to sin (43–47). Fire is introduced with the notion of being in hell, "where the worm does not die and the fire is not extinguished" (48), a quotation of Isa 66:24. After this comes the saying about salt. The version in Bezae recalls Lev 2:13,

---

o. Ibid.
p. A 5th century manuscript (A, 02).
q. Metzger, *A Textual Commentary on the Greek New Testament*, 87.

"Also all of your grain offerings you must season with salt; you must not omit the salt of your God's covenant from your offering," focusing on the salt and recalling sacrifice. The canonical version instead focuses on the believer and foresees persecution (fire).

Parallels

As mentioned above, the version in Bezae may be a recollection of Lev 2:13. Evans notes that Ezek 43:24 mentions similar things (salt and burnt offering).[r]

Translation

For every sacrifice will be salted with salt. (Mk 9:49 Brannan)

MARK 16:14 (WASHINGTONIANUS)

This interpolation, also known as the "Freer Logion"[s] is found in Codex Washingtonianus, a fourth or fifth-century Gospel codex. It occurs after Mark 16:14, in which the eleven disciples are rebuked for unbelief. The Freer Logion provides the disciples a chance to explain their unbelief, and for the risen Christ to explain more about his task and the gospel. Verse 15 follows, with Christ exhorting the disciples to "go into all the world and preach the gospel to all creation."

Parallels

There are no close parallels to this agraphon.

Translation

They offered this excuse: "This lawless and faithless age is under Satan, who does not allow what is unclean and dominated by spirits to grasp the true power of God. Therefore," they said to Christ, "reveal your just authority now." Christ replied: "The measure of the years of Satan's power has been fulfilled, but other terrible things are imminent. Yet it was for the sake of sinners that I was handed over to death, that they might return to

---

r. Craig A. Evans, *Mark 8:27–16:20*, Word Biblical Commentary 34B (Nashville: Thomas Nelson, 2001), 72.

s. Charles Freer purchased the manuscript in 1906. It is presently housed in the Freer Gallery of Art of the Smithsonian Institute in Washington, D.C.

the truth and sin no more, and inherit the spiritual and immortal glory of justification in heaven." (Mk 16:14 NAB)

LUKE 6:4 (BEZAE)

Luke 6:1–5 is the account of Jesus and his disciples picking and eating heads of grain on the Sabbath. The Pharisees interrupt with their accusation (2) and Jesus responds (3–4), noting David's eating of the bread of presentation. In Bezae, this agraphon comes next. Verse 5 ends with Jesus proclaiming the Son of Man as "Lord of the Sabbath," but Bezae moves verse 5 to follow verse 10, which has the effect of including Luke's account of the man with the withered hand (6–10) as the third example of Jesus' lordship over the Sabbath in a single group.[t]

Parallels

There are no close parallels to this agraphon. Fitzmyer notes some similarity with *Gos. Thom.* 3, 14.[u]

Translation

That same day, seeing someone working on the Sabbath, he said to him, "Man, if you know what you do, you are blessed. But if you do not know, you are a curse and a transgressor of the law." (Luke 6:4 Brannan)

LUKE 10:16 (BEZAE)

The larger pericope is Luke 10:1–20, the appointing and sending out of the 72 disciples. Jesus appoints the 72, gives them instructions, and sends them out (1–12). He issues woes to Chorazin and Bethsaida for their lack of repentance (13–14), and then similarly condemns Capernaum (15). Then he returns to the 72, stating "The one who listens to you listens to me, and the one who rejects you rejects me." In the standard edition, the rejection of Jesus is extended to a rejection of the one who sent Jesus; instead, in Bezae the heeding of Jesus is extended into also heeding the one who sent Jesus. This changes the focus of the section from negative (rejecting Jesus) to

---

t. Metzger, *A Textual Commentary on the Greek New Testament*, 117.

u. Joseph A. Fitzmyer, *The Gospel According to Luke I—IX: Introduction, Translation, and Notes*, Anchor Bible 28 (Garden City, NY: Doubleday, 1970), 609.

positive (heeding Jesus). Some other manuscripts append the ending found in Bezae onto what is considered the standard text, covering both options.[v]

Parallels

Similar statements by Jesus found in the gospels include Matt 10:40; John 5:23; 12:44–45; 13:20.[w]

Justin uses similar language in 1 *Apol.* 16.10 and 63.5.[x]

Translation

"But the one who hears me hears the one who sent me." (Lk 10:16 Brannan)

JOHN 8:7, 10–11 (BEZAE)

The account found in Codex Bezae, while differing from the standard text, does not substantively change the understanding of the event. In verse 7, Bezae omits "him" after "asking." The larger changes are in verses 10–11. In verse 10, the standard text "said, 'Woman'" becomes "said to the woman." In verse 11, "And she said" becomes "And that woman said to him," while "Go and" becomes "Go away."

Parallels

There are no close parallels to this agraphon.

Translation

And when they persisted in asking, he straightened up and said to them, "The one of you without sin, let him first throw a stone at her." (John 8:7 Brannan)

And Jesus, straightening up, said to the woman, "Where are they? Does no one condemn you?" And that woman said to him, "Nobody, Lord." And Jesus said "Neither do I condemn you. Go away, from now on, sin no longer." (Jn 8:10–11 Brannan)

---

v. Stroker, *Extracanonical Sayings of Jesus*, 159. He notes Θ and Φ.

w. Ibid.

x. Ibid.

SAYINGS IN THE APOSTOLIC FATHERS

The writings collectively known as the "Apostolic Fathers" were originally composed between AD 90–220. They have been collected and published as a group since the late 17th century.[y] They are some of the earliest witnesses of the Christian church available outside the writings of the New Testament.

These writings use both the Septuagint and the New Testament as sources of authority. At times, however, the authors appeal to sayings of Jesus not found within the canonical sources. These sayings are located in the following:

- 1 Clement 13.2

- 2 Clement 3.2

- 2 Clement 4.2

- 2 Clement 4.5

- 2 Clement 5.2–4

- 2 Clement 8.5

- 2 Clement 12.2–6

- 2 Clement 13.2

- 2 Clement 13.4

- Epistle of Barnabas 7.11

Each of these will be discussed below. The English translation of each passage is by the author.[z]

1 CLEMENT 13.2

The document known as 1 *Clement* is a letter from the church in Rome to the church in Corinth that urges the leaders of the Corinthian church to return expelled leaders to their roles in order to restore peace to the church. In

---

y. Wilhelm Pratscher, *The Apostolic Fathers: An Introduction* (Waco, TX: Baylor University Press, 2010), 1–2.

z. Rick Brannan, *The Apostolic Fathers in English* (Bellingham, WA: Lexham Press, 2017).

the sections before this agraphon, the author has reviewed the faith, hospitality and godliness of Enoch (1 *Clem.* 9.3), Noah (9.4), Abraham (10.1–7), Lot (11.1–2) and Rahab (12.1–8), urging the Corinthians to follow the pattern of godliness established by these luminaries. Section 13 follows,[aa] urging humility and the putting aside of anger and arrogance. *First Clement* 13.1 puts a pastiche of OT and NT material (Jer 9:23-24; 1 Sam 2:10; 1 Cor 1:31; 2 Cor 10:17) into the mouth of the Holy Spirit, then urges the reader to remember "the words of the Lord Jesus." The saying of Jesus to remember follows in verse 2, and it is the essence of the message of Rome to Corinth: "treat the leaders you expelled as you would like to be treated."

The Oxford Committee breaks the quotation into seven parts, noting near parallels for each part where available and recognizing that parts of the whole are not extant in the canonical gospels.[ab] Regarding the whole, they report:

> We incline to think that we have in Clem. Rom. a citation from some written or unwritten form of 'Catechesis' as to our Lord's teaching, current in the Roman Church, perhaps a local form which may go back to a time before our Gospels existed.[ac]

Klauck, however, attributes the source to a pre-written oral tradition:

> ... in view of the early date of this text, its author is probably still drawing directly on the oral tradition about Jesus, rather than using the Gospel of Matthew as his immediate source.[ad]

Whatever the source, this agraphon, attributed as it is to Jesus, gives extra authority and urgency to the message of the church of Rome to the church of Corinth.

---

aa. Robert M. Grant and Holt H. Graham, *First and Second Clement*, The Apostolic Fathers: A New Translation and Commentary 2 (New York: Thomas Nelson & Sons, 1965), 35–36. They see §13 as starting a new major section of the letter's argument.

ab. Oxford Society of Historical Theology, *The New Testament in the Apostolic Fathers* (Oxford: Oxford University Press, 1905), 58–61.

ac. Ibid., 61.

ad. Klauck, *Apocryphal Gospels*, 11.

Parallels

Similarities to the canonical gospels include Matt 5:7; 6:14–15; 7:1–2, 12; Luke 6:31, 36–38; each of which record material similar to some portion of Clement's larger saying.

Parallels in noncanonical material include Polycarp, *Phil.* 2.3; Clement of Alexandria, *Strom.* 2.18.91; and *Apos. Con.* 2.21, 36, 42.[ae]

Translation

For he spoke as follows: "Show mercy, that you may be shown mercy; forgive, that it may be forgiven you; as you do so will it be done to you; as you give so will it be given to you; as you judge so will you be judged; as you are kind so will kindness be shown to you; with which measure you measure, with it will be measured to you." (1Cl 13.2 Brannan)

2 CLEMENT 3.2

Second Clement, which in all likelihood was not written by the same author as 1 *Clement*, is the earliest known non-canonical example of a Christian homily (sermon). It is largely based on Isa 54 and is an exhortation to Christians to do what is right.[af]

The first two sections of 2 *Clem.* introduce what God saved his people from (a fog of darkness, called from non-being into being, 2 *Clem.* 1.6–8) and what God wants his people to do (save the perishing, 2.5–6). Next comes a question: How does the Christian acknowledge and respond to God's mercy (3.1)? The agraphon in 3.2 answers this question: the one who acknowledges the Lord before men will be acknowledged before God in heaven. This agraphon is similar to canonical material (Matt 10:32; Luke 12:8) and may be a restating or recollection of canonical material, but it is different enough to reflect a different source.[ag] Either way, the saying is used in an authoritative manner to direct the reader/hearer to action, with 2 *Clem.* 3.3–5 explicitly directing one how to acknowledge the Lord among people.

---

ae. Stroker, *Extracanonical Sayings of Jesus*, 198–200; Oxford Society of Historical Theology, *The New Testament in the Apostolic Fathers*, 58–61.

af. Pratscher, *The Apostolic Fathers*, 77–85.

ag. Oxford Society of Historical Theology, *The New Testament in the Apostolic Fathers*, 130.

Parallels

Parallels in canonical material include Matt 10:32; Luke 12:8.

Translation

And he himself also says, "The one who confesses me before people, I will confess him before my Father." (2Cl 3.2 Brannan)

2 CLEMENT 4.2

The author of 2 *Clem.*, after quoting Isa 29:13, proceeds to discuss true acknowledgment of the Lord.[ah] Simply saying the name will not save (2 *Clem.* 4.1). This agraphon (4.2) is used to indicate the depth of confession and necessity of practice. It uses the saying to reinforce what Isa 29:13 has introduced, that the Christian must confess with both mouth and heart, and that actions give witness to the confession of the heart.

Parallels

This saying is similar to Matt 7:21, but much abridged and generalized.[ai] It may be a recollection of canonical material, but it could also reflect alternate material, particularly given the proximity of other sayings that are similar to, yet different from, canonical material (2 *Clem.* 3.2; 4.5, 5.2–4).[aj]

Translation

For he says, "Not everyone who says to me, 'Lord, Lord!' will be saved, but the one who practices righteousness." (2Cl 4.2 Brannan)

2 CLEMENT 4.5

After clarifying that both right confession and right action are necessary,[ak] the author of 2 *Clem.* provides an answer to the question of those who confess the Lord with their mouths but act contrary to their confession (2 *Clem.* 4.3–4). The answer is that they will be thrown out; they will no longer be acknowledged before God (5).

---

ah. See comments on 2 *Clem.* 3.2 on "true acknowledgment."
ai. Stroker, *Extracanonical Sayings of Jesus*, 71.
aj. Oxford Society of Historical Theology, *The New Testament in the Apostolic Fathers*, 131.
ak. See comments on 2 *Clem.* 4.2.

Parallels

Canonical parallels are found in Matt 7:23; 25:12; Luke 13:27; Psa 6:8.

What has been called the "Gospel of the Nazaraeans"[al] also has a parallel, in section 5.[am]

Translation

Because of this, you who do these things, the Lord said, "If you have gathered with me in my bosom and you do not do my commandments, I will throw you out and I will say to you, 'Leave me! I do not know where you are from, you doers of iniquity!'" (2Cl 4.5 Brannan)

2 CLEMENT 5.2–4

After discussing the necessity and benefit of acknowledging God (2 *Clem.* 4), the author of 2 *Clem.* discusses what may happen to those who acknowledge God (5.1). A lengthy discussion between Jesus and Peter is included, based on Luke 10:3; 12:4–5; and Matt 10:16, 28. The agraphon removes the focus from what may happen in this world (wolves devouring sheep, 2–3) to what may happen in the next world (destruction of soul and body in the hell of fire, 4). In the agraphon, Peter's focus is shifted from temporal to eternal; the reader's focus is intended to shift similarly.

Parallels

Canonical parallels are found in Luke 10:3; 12:4–5; and Matt 10:16, 28.

Parallels to 2 *Clem.* 5.2 are found in Prochorus, *Acts of John* 83 and *The Epistle of Pseudo-Titus* 80.[an] P.Oxy. 4009[ao] contains this same agraphon, only with Peter in the first person singular, possibly indicating that this agraphon has the *Gospel of Peter* as its source.

Translation

For the Lord said, "You will be like sheep among wolves." And answering, Peter said to him, "But if the wolves tear apart the sheep?" Jesus said to

---

al. Philipp Vielhauer and Georg Strecker, "IV. Jewish-Christian Gospels," in *New Testament Apocrypha*, rev. ed. (Louisville: Westminster John Knox, 1991), 1:154–165.

am. Stroker, *Extracanonical Sayings of Jesus*, 70.

an. Ibid., 17–18.

ao. See comments on P.Oxy. 4009 in discussion of the *Gospel of Peter*.

Peter, "The sheep have no fear of the wolves after they are dead, and you have no fear of those who kill you and who are able to do nothing more to you, but you fear him who after you are dead has power to throw soul and body into the hell of fire." (2Cl 5.2–4 Brannan)

2 CLEMENT 8.5

Second Clement 8 begins with a call to repentance (2 *Clem.* 8.1). It is followed by the example of clay in the hand of a potter, noting that the clay is malleable before it is fired in the kiln, but impossible to shape after being fired. This example is extended to the audience as an exhortation to repent while there is still time (2) because after departing from the world, there will be no more time for confession or repentance (3). Repenting before then is equated with eternal life (4), and this view is justified with appeal to the agraphon, specifically quoted as from "the gospel" (5), likely relating the agraphon to the material found in Luke 16:10–12 (small and big) with an expanded application (least important and very important).[ap] The sense of the saying is changed from its canonical use—where it is an encouragement to the disciples Jesus is sending out—into an encouragement where the "least important" are things of this world and the "very important" are the things of heaven, eternal life. This is clarified in 2 *Clem.* 8.6: "Therefore he means this: keep the flesh pure and the seal unstained in order that we may receive eternal life."

Parallels

The canonical parallel is Luke 16:10–12. A similar saying is found in Irenaeus, *Haer.* 2.23.3.[aq]

Translation

For the Lord says in the gospel, "If you did not guard the small things, who will give you the big things? For I say to you that whoever is faithful with the least important is also faithful with the very important." (2Cl 8.5 Brannan)

---

ap. Helmut Koester, "The Extracanonical Sayings of the Lord as Products of the Christian Community," in *The Historical Jesus and the Rejected Gospels*, ed. Charles W. Hedrick, Semeia 44 (Atlanta: Scholars Press, 1988), 63.

aq. Stroker, *Extracanonical Sayings of Jesus*, 119–120.

2 CLEMENT 12.2–6

The section begins with a call to wait and watch for the kingdom of God because the timing of its arrival is unknown (12.1). The agraphon occurs next, with an appeal to "the Lord himself" as source, as the authoritative answer to the question of the kingdom's arrival. Following the agraphon (3–6) the author provides a full explanation and commentary on the saying so that the meaning cannot be misunderstood.[ar]

Parallels

There are no clear canonical parallels. Similar material is found in Clement, *Strom.* 3.13.92, where it is attributed to the "Gospel of the Egyptians." An expanded form is found in *Gos. Thom.* 22.[as]

Translation

For when the Lord himself was asked by someone when his kingdom will come, he said, "When the two shall be one, and the outside as the inside, and the male with the female neither male nor female."And "the two are one" when we speak the truth with ourselves, and there is one soul in two bodies with no hypocrisy. And "the outside as the inside" means this: "the inside" means the soul and "the outside" means the body. Therefore in this manner your body is made visible, so also let your soul be evident in good works. And "the male with the female neither male nor female" means this: that a brother, upon seeing a sister, thinks nothing about her being a female, nor does she think anything about him being a male. When you do these things, he says, the kingdom of my Father will come. (2Cl 12.2–6 Brannan)

2 CLEMENT 13.2

Again, a call to repentance commences the section (2 *Clem.* 13.1), adding a warning against blasphemy. Then comes a quotation from Isa 52:5, "My name is blasphemed continually among all the nations" (2). To this agraphon, a woe statement, is added. The woe statement reinforces the warning against blasphemy, providing a consequence for the act. The source of the

---

ar. It seems even in the time of 2 *Clem.*, people were saying and believing crazy things about the timing of the Lord's return.

as. Stroker, *Extracanonical Sayings of Jesus*, 12.

woe statement in 2 *Clem.* is "the Lord" but as the first quotation is a reference to Isaiah, the direct tie to Jesus as speaker is uncertain.

Further, woe to the blasphemer is a common theme (*e.g.* Ign. *Trall.* 8.2;
Pol. *Phil.* 10.3), and its origin is uncertain. Lightfoot considers this agraphon to be a restatement of Isa 52:5.[at] Schoedel, in his commentary on the
letters of Ignatius, provides more insight:

> It is likely that the passage first belonged to a collection of biblical
> testimonies against the Jews and was then adopted for paraenetic
> purposes. For there are two forms of the verse—one close to the bib-
> lical text and the other prefaced (as in *Tr.* 8.2) by a "woe" (Pol. *Phil.*
> 10.3; 2 *Clem.* 13.2; *Const. Apost.* 1.10; 3.5); and it seems unlikely that all
> the passages which diverge from the Bible go back to Ignatius. Note
> in particular (a) that 2 *Clement* provides both forms of the passage
> and treats them as distinct verses of the Bible (13.2–4).... Thus it
> is likely that the woe-form of Isa 52:5 arose under the influence of
> other verses traditionally associated with it in a collection of texts.[au]

While this saying may not tie Jesus directly to its source, it is used with
divine authority to reinforce the author's warning against blasphemy.

Parallels

Canonical parallels include Isa 52:5 and Rom 2:24. Further parallels include
Ign. *Trall.* 8.2;[av] Pol. *Phil.* 10.3; *Apos. Con.* 1.10; 3.5; Justin *Dial.* 17.2.[aw]

Translation

For the Lord says, "My name is blasphemed continually among all the
nations," and again "Woe to him on account of whom my name is blasphemed."How is it blasphemed? By you who do not do what I desire. (2Cl
13.2 Brannan)

---

at. J. B. Lightfoot, *The Apostolic Fathers Part 1, S. Clement of Rome,* 2nd ed. (London:
Macmillan, 1890), 2:242.

au. William Schoedel, *Ignatius of Antioch: A Commentary on the Letters of Ignatius of Antioch,*
ed. Helmut Koester, Hermeneia (Philadelphia: Fortress, 1985), 150.

av. Lightfoot, *S. Clement of Rome,* 2:242.

aw. Schoedel, *Ignatius of Antioch,* 150.

2 CLEMENT 13.4

After the possible agraphon in 2 *Clem.* 13.2,[ax] the author notes a problem with those who hear of the sayings of God but later learn "our works not are worthy of the words which we speak" (3) and turn to blasphemy because of the disconnect between the words and works of those who claim to be Christian. From here, the author gives the agraphon as an example, quoting what "God says" and including a saying reminiscent of Luke 6:32, 35.[ay] The agraphon authoritatively sets forth the teaching that Christians must reflect, but the author shows the disparity between words and actions that leads to blasphemy on the part of those outside the Christian community.

Parallels

Canonical parallels include Luke 6:32, 35.

Translation

For when they hear from us that God says, "It is no credit to you if you love those who love you, but it is a credit to you if you love your enemies and those who hate you."When they hear these things, they are astonished at the extraordinary degree of goodness, but when they see that not only do we not love those who hate us, but that not even those who love us, they laugh at us and the name is blasphemed. (2Cl 13.4 Brannan)

EPISTLE OF BARNABAS 7.11

The *Epistle of Barnabas* is a pseudepigraphal and allegorical investigation of Scripture.[az] The larger context of *Barn.* 7 is a discussion of the suffering of the Messiah and an examination of how Jesus typologically fulfills prophecies. In *Barn.* 7.6–11, the author cites the example of the scapegoat (Lev 16:7–10) and discusses how Jesus in his crucifixion fulfilled the role of the scapegoat. He ends the section (11) with the agraphon. The larger context is helpful here in understanding the role the agraphon plays in providing authority for the argument.

---

ax. See above comments on 2 *Clem.* 13.2.

ay. Lightfoot, *S. Clement of Rome*, 2:243.

az. Rick Brannan, "Apostolic Fathers," in *Lexham Bible Dictionary*, ed. John D. Barry, et al. (Bellingham, WA: Logos Bible Software, 2012–2015).

For how is he like that goat? For this reason: "The goats are similar, beautiful and equal," so that when they see him, then upon coming, they will be greatly astounded by the likeness of the goat. See then the type of Jesus who was destined to suffer. But why is it that the wool is put in the middle of the thorns? It is a type of Jesus placed in the church, because whoever desires to take away the scarlet wool, it is necessary for him to suffer many things because the thorns are terrible and can gain it only through affliction. Thus he says, "Those who desire to see me and to take hold of my kingdom must take hold of me through affliction and suffering."[ba]

The author establishes a link between suffering and the scapegoat, and between Jesus and the scapegoat. The agraphon links the one who follows Jesus to the affliction and suffering foreshadowed, according to the author, by the scapegoat.

While the agraphon does put these words into the mouth of Jesus, most scholars consider the source to be the author himself.[bb] Koester notes, "As Barnabas interprets the entire sacrificial rite typologically, such a saying of Jesus can arise from the Jewish prototype without any special effort."[bc]

Parallels

Stroker cites Prochorus, *Acts of John* 83 as an associated text, as well as 4 *Ezra* 7:14 and Irenaeus, *Haer.* 5.28.3.[bd]

Translation

But why is it that the wool is put in the middle of the thorns? It is a type of Jesus placed in the church, because whoever desires to take away the scarlet wool, it is necessary for him to suffer many things because the thorns are terrible and can gain it only through affliction. Thus he says, "Those who desire to see me and to take hold of my kingdom must take hold of me through affliction and suffering." (Barn 7.11 Brannan)

---

ba. Brannan, *The Apostolic Fathers in English* (*Barn.* 7.10–11).

bb. Klauck, *Apocryphal Gospels*, 12; Oxford Society of Historical Theology, *The New Testament in the Apostolic Fathers*, 21.

bc. Koester, "The Extracanonical Sayings," 68.

bd. Stroker, *Extracanonical Sayings of Jesus*, 84–85.

SAYINGS IN JUSTIN MARTYR

Justin Martyr (c. AD 100–c.165) was a pagan philosopher who converted to Christianity c.130.[be] He was "the most significant of the second century apologists for Christianity."[bf] One of his books, the *Dialogue with Trypho*, was an effort to convince Trypho (a Jew) that post-Christian Jews had excised pro-Christian material from their books.[bg] This book contains two possible agrapha.

- Dialogue with Trypho 35.3

- Dialogue with Trypho 47.5

The Greek text used is that of Trollope;[bh] English translation is by the author unless otherwise stated.

DIALOGUE WITH TRYPHO 35.3

This agraphon, found in §35 of the *Dialogue*, occurs in a section where Trypho brings up the issue of heretics confessing to be believers. For Trypho, this is a problem. How can one who does things opposed to Christianity also confess it? In response, Justin acknowledges the problem and says it motivates true Christians all the more. Then Justin notes that Jesus Christ predicted such things: "For what things he predicted would take place in his name, these we do see being actually accomplished in his sight."[bi] The agraphon follows this introduction, confirming (for Justin) that Jesus predicted such things, so they are to be expected.

Some note the similarity to 1 Cor 11:18 and posit that this is actually a saying of Paul that was transformed into a saying of Jesus.[bj]

---

be. F. L. Cross and E. A. Livingstone, eds., *The Oxford Dictionary of the Christian Church*, 3rd rev. ed. (Oxford: Oxford University Press, 2005), 920.

bf. Robert M. Grant, "Justin Martyr," *ABD* 3:1133.

bg. Ibid., 3:1133–34.

bh. W. Trollope, *S. Justini Philosophi et Martyris cum Tryphone Judaeo Dialogus. Pars Prior, Colloquium Primi Diei Continens. Edited, with a Corrected Text and English Introductions and Notes*, Vol. 1 (Cambridge: J.Hall, 1846).

bi. Alexander Roberts, James Donaldson, and A. Cleveland Coxe, eds., *The Apostolic Fathers with Justin Martyr and Irenaeus*, ANF 1 (Buffalo, NY: Christian Literature Company, 1885), 212.

bj. Klauck, *Apocryphal Gospels*, 13–14.

Parallels

Canonical parallels to this saying include Matt 24:5; 7:15; as well as 1 Cor 11:18. Parallels are also found in *Didaskalia* 6.5; Didymus, *De Trinitate* 3.22.[bk]

Translation

For he said, "Many shall come in my name outwardly clothed with sheep skins, but within they are ravening wolves." And, "There shall be schisms and heresies." (*Dial.* 35.3 James)

Dialogue with Trypho 47.5

In this section of the *Dialogue*, Trypho asks Justin if those who confess Christ but who are also observant of the law will be saved. Justin answers affirmatively, but qualifies it only as his own opinion. Trypho pushes further, inquiring about the disagreement implied by Justin's answer. Justin uses Trypho's further inquiry to examine the relationship between Jews and Christians. Justin's position is that those Jews who confess Christ must not compel other Christians to circumcision, Sabbath-keeping, and the like, but also affirms that Jews who confess Christ will be saved. At the very end of this discussion, Justin appeals to this agraphon. He uses it to authenticate his position that Christ will save those who confess Him, despite their state at the time of confession.

Despite the clarity of Justin's citation of this text as a saying of Jesus, there are questions as to its origin. Baker writes: "This saying is a well-known example of those uncanonical phrases that are not found in any NT manuscript, either as text or marginal gloss, but are very frequently cited in Christian literature."[bl] His study is the most wide-ranging, but firm conclusions regarding the source are simply not possible. Baker notes, "A saying once made can easily be repeated after the elliptical 'he said' and become confused with the utterances of Jesus.... It is not impossible that this has happened in our case."[bm] Others have supposed this saying as coming from a non-extant apocryphal gospel according to the Hebrews,[bn]

---

bk. Stroker, *Extracanonical Sayings of Jesus*, 72–73.
bl. A. Baker, "Justin's Agraphon in the Dialogue with Trypho," *JBL* 87 (1968): 277.
bm. Ibid., 287.
bn. Ibid.

from the apocryphal book of Ezekiel,[bo] or as a Christianized gloss from the canonical book of Ezekiel.[bp]

Parallels

There are no direct canonical parallels to this agraphon. There are later parallels, including *Liber Graduum* 15.4 and 3.3; Clement of Alexandria, *Quis div.* 40; Ps. Athanasius, *Quaestiones ad Antiochum* 36.[bq]

Translation

Therefore also our Lord Jesus Christ said, "In whatever state I lay hold of you, in this state I will also judge you." (*Dial.* 47.5 Brannan)

SELECT BIBLIOGRAPHY

Baker, A. "Justin's Agraphon in the Dialogue with Trypho." *Journal of Biblical Literature* 87 (1968): 277–87.

Brannan, Rick. "Apostolic Fathers." In *Lexham Bible Dictionary*. Edited by John D. Barry, et al. Bellingham, WA: Logos Bible Software, 2012–2015.

———. *The Apostolic Fathers in English*. Bellingham, WA: Lexham Press, 2017.

Confraternity of Christian Doctrine, Board of Trustees, Catholic Church, National Conference of Catholic Bishops, and United States Catholic Conference. *The New American Bible: Translated from the Original Languages With Critical Use of All the Ancient Sources and Revised New Testament*. Washington, D. C.: Confraternity of Christian Doctrine, 1996.

Cross, F. L., and E. A. Livingstone, eds. *The Oxford Dictionary of the Christian Church*. 3rd rev. ed. Oxford: Oxford University Press, 2005.

Crossan, John Dominic. *Four Other Gospels: Shadows on the Contours of Canon*. New York: Harper & Row, 1985.

---

bo. Ibid., 277.
bp. Ibid., 286.
bq. Stroker, Extracanonical Sayings of Jesus, 73.

————. *The Cross That Spoke: The Origins of the Passion Narrative.* San Francisco: Harper & Row, 1988.

Ehrman, Bart D., and Zlatko Pleše. *The Apocryphal Gospels: Texts and Translations.* Oxford: Oxford University Press, 2010.

Evans, Craig A. *Mark 8:27–16:20.* Edited by Ralph P. Martin and Lynn A. Losie. WBC 34B. Nashville: Thomas Nelson, 2001.

————. "The Life of Jesus." Pages 427–75 in *Handbook to the Exegesis of the New Testament.* Edited by S. E. Porter. New Testament Tools and Studies 25. Leiden: Brill, 1997.

Fitzmyer, Joseph A. *The Acts of the Apostles: A New Translation with Introduction and Commentary.* Anchor Bible 31. New York: Doubleday, 1998.

————. *The Gospel According to Luke I—IX: Introduction, Translation, and Notes.* Anchor Bible 28. Garden City, NY: Doubleday, 1970.

Grant, Robert M., and Holt H. Graham. *First and Second Clement.* The Apostolic Fathers: A New Translation and Commentary 2. New York: Thomas Nelson & Sons, 1965.

Grant, Robert M. "Justin Martyr." *ABD* 3:1133–34.

Harris III, W. Hall, Elliot Ritzema, Rick Brannan, Douglas Mangum, Jeffrey A. Reimer, and Micah Wierenga, eds. *The Lexham English Bible.* Bellingham, WA: Logos Bible Software, 2012.

Hofius, O. "Isolated Sayings of the Lord." Pages 88–91 in vol. 1 of *New Testament Apocrypha.* Rev. ed. Edited by Wilhelm Schneemelcher. Translated by R. McL. Wilson. 2 vols. Louisville: Westminster John Knox, 1991.

James, M. R. *The Apocryphal New Testament.* Oxford: Clarendon, 1924.

Klauck, Hans-Josef. *Apocryphal Gospels: An Introduction.* London: T&T Clark, 2004.

Koester, Helmut. "The Extracanonical Sayings of the Lord as Products of the Christian Community." Pages 57–77 in *The Historical Jesus and the Rejected Gospels.* Edited by Charles W. Hedrick. Semeia 44. Atlanta: Scholars Press, 1988.

Lightfoot, J. B. *The Apostolic Fathers Part 1, S. Clement of Rome.* 2 vols. 2nd ed. London: Macmillan, 1890.

Metzger, Bruce M., ed. *A Textual Commentary on the Greek New Testament.* 2nd rev. ed. New York: United Bible Societies, 1994.

Oxford Society of Historical Theology. *The New Testament in the Apostolic Fathers*. Oxford: Oxford, 1905.

Pratscher, Wilhelm. *The Apostolic Fathers: An Introduction*. Waco, TX: Baylor University Press, 2010.

Roberts, Alexander, James Donaldson, and A. Cleveland Coxe, eds. *The Apostolic Fathers with Justin Martyr and Irenaeus*. ANF 1. Buffalo, NY: Christian Literature Company, 1885.

Schoedel, William. *Ignatius of Antioch: A Commentary on the Letters of Ignatius of Antioch*. Edited by Helmut Koester. Hermeneia. Philadelphia: Fortress, 1985.

Stroker, William D. "Agrapha." *ABD* 1:92–95.

———. *Extracanonical Sayings of Jesus*. Society of Biblical Literature, 1989.

Trollope, W. S. *Justini Philosophi et Martyris cum Tryphone Judaeo Dialogus. Pars Prior, Colloquium Primi Diei Continens. Edited, with a Corrected Text and English Introductions and Notes*. Vol. 1. 2 vols. Cambridge: J. Hall, 1846.

Vielhauer, Philipp, and Georg Strecker. "IV. Jewish-Christian Gospels." Pages 134–78 in Vol. 1 of *New Testament Apocrypha*. Edited by Wilhelm Schneemelcher. Translated by R. McL. Wilson. 2 vols. Louisville: Westminster John Knox, 1991.

Yamauchi, E. M. "Agrapha." *ISBE* 1:69–71.

— The Protevangelium of James

INTRODUCTION

The *Protevangelium of James* (or "Proto-Gospel," *Prot. Jas.*) is a story that focuses on Mary the mother of Jesus, providing a history for her and her family. Like many people today, early Christians understood the basics of human reproduction and were confused about how Mary could be the mother of Jesus with no earthly human father. The *Protevangelium of James* was meant to assuage concerns among early Christian believers by providing assurances about this and other aspects of Jesus' birth.

It is thought to have originated between AD 150 and 200, largely because of quotations found in early writers such as Clement of Alexandria, Origen, and perhaps even Justin Martyr.[a] The *Protevangelium of James* is thought to have been written in Greek; the earliest available Greek manuscript is dated to the fourth century.[b] It must have had lasting popularity; there are several later manuscripts in Greek (10th–17th centuries), as well as versions in Syriac, Armenian, Coptic, Ethiopic, and even Georgian.[c]

Because of the relatively large amount of manuscript evidence, the Greek text of *Prot. Jas.* is eclectic, not a transcription of a single manuscript. Most modern English translations are based on the text of Tischendorf,[d] although some (such as Ehrman and Pleše)[e] are based on de Strycker's edition.[f]

---

a. Willem S. Vorster, "James, Protevangelium of," *ABD* 3:630.
b. Ibid.
c. Bart D. Ehrman and Zlatko Pleše, *The Apocryphal Gospels: Texts and Translations* (Oxford: Oxford University Press, 2010), 36.
d. C. von Tischendorf, *Evangelia Apocrypha*, 2nd ed. (Leipzig: Mendelssohn, 1876), 1–50.
e. Ehrman and Pleše, *The Apocryphal Gospels*, 35.
f. É. de Strycker, *La forme la plus ancienne du Protévangile de Jacques* (Brussels: Société des Bollandistes, 1961).

Content

The early part of *Prot. Jas.* contains several parallels between Mary and the story of Hannah, the mother of Samuel (1 Sam 1-4). Mary's parents, Joachim and Anna, are childless. Joachim is a prominent rich man; he freely gives gifts (sacrifices) for himself and for other people. However, because he is childless, he is no longer able to give out of his excess for the people. This grieves him; he separates himself and goes into the wilderness for 40 days (*Prot. Jas.* 1).

Anna is also grieved about her childlessness, and she mourns during these 40 days (*Prot. Jas.* 2-3). During this time, an angel appears and tells her that she will bear a child (*Prot. Jas.* 4). She responds by saying the child will be devoted to the Lord. She is told that Joachim received a similar vision, and that he will be arriving home soon.

In due time, Anna gives birth to a daughter, Mary. Mary lives with Anna and Joachim for three years before she is given to the temple, as Anna promised (*Prot. Jas.* 5-7).

When Mary turns 12, the priests decide it is time for her to leave, as her budding womanhood presents the possibility of defiling the temple. They seek a guardian for her and the lot falls to Joseph, a widower with adult sons, who is a contractor. Despite his protests, Mary is delivered into his custody, and she returns with him to his home (*Prot. Jas.* 8-10).

While Joseph is away on business, an angel approaches Mary to tell her she will conceive "of the word" of the "Master of all things" (*Prot. Jas.* 11.2). After a trip to the temple, Mary visits her cousin Elizabeth, pregnant with John the Baptist, and stays there three months. At the end of her visit, she is six months pregnant (*Prot. Jas.* 12).

Joseph returns from his trip to find Mary six months pregnant. He goes into shock, worried about his standing among the people and before God (*Prot. Jas.* 13). An angel appears to him, confirming Mary's story that she is indeed pure and undefiled (*Prot. Jas.* 14). Priests then question Mary and Joseph about their story. Tests administered by the priests (compare Num 5:11-31) indicate that Mary and Joseph are telling the truth, so they are left alone (*Prot. Jas.* 15-16).

The census ordered by Caesar Augustus (compare Luke 2:1-3) causes Mary and Joseph to travel to Bethlehem. Along the way, Mary indicates the child is coming and cannot be prevented. Joseph finds a cave, and Mary stays in the cave while Joseph looks for a midwife. He finds a midwife immediately, and she assists with the birth (*Prot. Jas.* 17–19). The midwife goes out of the cave and meets a woman named Salome. Salome, doubting Mary's virginity, tests her after the birth and finds that she is indeed a virgin. As a result of her test Salome's hand is burned to the point of nearly falling off (*Prot. Jas.* 20), but her hand is miraculously restored after she picks up the baby Jesus.

The magi arrive in Judea, seeking the king of the Jews. After meeting with Herod, they leave, find the child in the cave with Mary and Joseph, and offer gifts. They return to their own land by another route (*Prot. Jas.* 21). When he realizes that the magi tricked him, Herod orders the murder of children under two years old.[g] Both Mary and Elizabeth (John the Baptist's mother) are able to keep their children from being subject to the infanticide, although Zacharias (John's father) is killed in the temple because he did not tell Herod's men where his son was hidden (*Prot. Jas.* 22–24).

The book ends with testimony from James that he is the one who wrote it (*Prot. Jas.* 25).

Relationship to the New Testament

There are several points in *Prot. Jas.* that allude to the story of Jesus' birth as known in from the New Testament. Stanley Porter notes the following areas of verbal similarity:[h]

- *Prot. Jas.* 11.2–9 == Luke 1:28–42

- *Prot. Jas.* 12.2, 5 == Luke 1:43–44, 46

- *Prot. Jas.* 21.9–11 == Matt 2:8–11

- *Prot. Jas.* 22.1 == Matt 2:16

- *Prot. Jas.* 22.2 == Luke 2:7

---

g. Matt 2:16–18

h. Stanley E. Porter, "Early Apocryphal Gospels and the New Testament Text," in *The Early Text of the New Testament*, ed. Charles E. Hill and Michael J. Kruger (Oxford: Oxford University Press, 2012), 366–68. Porter lists all phrases that have grammatical and contextual similarities, and his complete list is larger than what is represented here. Instead of listing all passages, some of which indicate only a few words in common, I have listed only portions that indicate larger ranges of similarity and consolidated where appropriate.

- *Prot. Jas.* 24.13–14 == Luke 2:25–26

The canonical stories of Jesus' birth form the outline of the story of Jesus' birth found in *Prot. Jas.* The source for the other details is unknown.

Distinctives

While there are many similarities between the accounts of Jesus' birth found in *Prot. Jas.* and the New Testament Gospels, there are also many differences. Among these are three miracles in *Prot. Jas.* worth noting.

The first is the stopping of time Joseph experiences in *Prot. Jas.* 18.2. After entering the cave with Mary, Joseph left to look for a midwife. Here the narrative switches to first person with Joseph as speaker. He says, "I was walking, yet I did not walk." Other people and objects are described in a similar state, but not moving: "there were sheep being driven, and they did not go forward but stood still; and the shepherd lifted his hand to strike them with his staff, yet his hand remained up." The picture is of a frozen moment. Joseph is caught in that moment but consciously aware of it. As quickly as the moment came, it left: "And suddenly all things were restored to their course." After this experience, Joseph locates a Hebrew midwife, and returns to the cave with her.

Another miraculous account occurs in the cave after Jesus is born (*Prot. Jas.* 19.2–20.4). The midwife leaves the cave and meets a woman named Salome. The midwife, unable to contain her excitement at what has just taken place, tells Salome about what she saw. Salome responds with the same doubt expressed by Thomas after Jesus' resurrection.[i] She says, "As the Lord my God lives, if I do not put in my finger and prove her nature I will not believe that a virgin has given birth" (19.3). Salome does exactly this; she goes to the cave and physically verifies Mary's virginity. The hand she used for the test is stricken as if burned to the point of falling off, and she is immediately repentant (20.1–2). After her repentance, an angel instructs her to pick up the baby Jesus and she will be healed. She follows the angel's instruction and is healed. Salome is then told to "tell no one of the wonders that you have seen, until the child enters into Jerusalem" (20.3–4).

---

i. John 20:24–29

A third miraculous account involves Elizabeth and her infant son, John the Baptist (*Prot. Jas.* 22.3). Herod has ordered the killing of the infants. Mary hides Jesus in swaddling clothes and puts him in a cattle trough (22.2).[j] Elizabeth runs to the hills with John, looking for a place to hide, but finds nowhere suitable. Exhausted, Elizabeth groans, "Mountain of God, receive a mother with her child." The mountain "split in two and took her in." Elizabeth and John are safe inside the mountain: "[the mountain] was shining a light on them, for an angel of the Lord was with them, keeping watch over them." (22.3).

TRANSLATION

The translation is a reworking of M. R. James' translation,[k] edited in consultation with Tischendorf's Greek text.[l]

1.1 In the histories of the twelve tribes of Israel there was *one* Joachim, *who was* exceedingly rich. And he offered his gifts in a double portion, saying, "That which is of my excess shall be for the whole people, and that which is for my forgiveness shall be for the Lord, for a propitiation for me."

2 Now the great day of the Lord drew near and the children[m] of Israel offered their gifts. And Reuben stood over against him saying, "It is not lawful for you to offer your gifts first, because ₁you have had no children₁[n] in Israel." 3 And Joachim was exceedingly grieved, and went to *the record* of the twelve tribes of the people, saying, "I will look upon *the record* of the twelve tribes of Israel, whether I only ₁have had no children₁[o] in Israel." And he searched, and found *concerning* all the righteous, that they ₁had children₁[p] in Israel. And he remembered the patriarch Abraham, how in the last days God gave him a son, even Isaac. 4 And Joachim was exceedingly grieved and did not appear to his wife, but ₁went alone₁[q] into the wilderness, and pitched his

---

j. Luke 2:7
k. M. R. James, *The Apocryphal New Testament* (Oxford: Clarendon, 1924), 38–49.
l. Tischendorf, *Evangelia Apocrypha*, 1–50.
m. Or "sons"
n. Literally "you have not produced seed"
o. Literally "have not produced seed"
p. Literally "had raised up seed"
q. Literally "took himself"

tent there, and fasted forty days and forty nights, saying to himself, "I will not go down either for meat or for drink until the Lord my God visits me, and my prayer shall be *like* meat and drink to me."

²·¹ Now his wife Anna lamented with two lamentations, and mourned with two cries of mourning, saying, "I will mourn my widowhood, and I will mourn my childlessness."

² And the great day of the Lord drew near, and Judith her handmaid said, "How long will you humble your soul? The great day of the Lord has come, and it is not lawful for you to mourn. But take this headband that the supervisor of my work gave me; yet it is not lawful for me to put it on, since I am a handmaid and it has a mark of royalty." ³ And Anna said, "Get away from me! I have done nothing and the Lord has greatly humbled me, lest perhaps *some* crafty person has given it to you, and you have come to make me an accomplice in your sin." And Judith said, "How can I curse you, seeing the Lord has closed your womb, to give you no fruit in Israel?"

⁴ And Anna was exceedingly grieved. And she took off her clothes of mourning and ₗwashed her faceⱼʳ and put on her bridal garments, and about the ninth hour she went down into the garden to walk there. And she saw a laurel tree and sat down underneath it and prayed the Master, saying, "O God of our fathers, bless me, and hear my prayer, just as you blessed the womb of Sarah, and gave her a son, Isaac."ˢ

³·¹ And looking up into the sky she saw a nest of sparrows in the laurel tree, and ₗgrievedⱼᵗ saying:

> "Woe *is* me; who gave me birth?
>   And what womb brought me forth?
>   For I have been born as a curse before the childrenᵘ of Israel,
>   and I am reproached,

---

r. Literally "cleansed her head"
s. Gen 21:1–7
t. Literally "made a lamentation within herself"
u. Or "sons"

and ₗthey have mocked₁ᵛ me from the temple of the Lord.

2 Woe *is* me; what am I like?
I am not like the birds of the sky,
for even the birds of the sky are fruitful before you,
    O Lord.

Woe *is* me; what am I like?
I am not like the beasts of the earth,
for even the beasts of the earth are fruitful before you,
    O Lord.

Woe *is* me; what am I like?
I am not like these waters,
for even these waters are fruitful before you, O Lord.

3 Woe *is* me; what am I like?
I am not like this earth,
for even this earth brings forth her fruits in due season
    and blesses you, O Lord."

4.1 And behold, an angel of the Lord appeared and said to her, "Anna, Anna, the Lord has heard your prayer, and you will conceive and give birth, and your seed will be spoken of throughout the whole world." And Anna said, "As the Lord my God lives, if I give birth to either ₗa boy or girl₁,ʷ I will bring the child for a gift to the Lord my God, and it will minister to him all the days of its life."ˣ

2 And behold, two angels came and said to her, "Behold, Joachim your husband comes with his flocks. For an angel of the Lord came down to him and said, 'Joachim, Joachim, the Lord God has heard your prayer. ₗGo home₁!ʸ For behold, your wife Anna ₗhas conceived₁.' "ᶻ 3 And Joachim went down and called his herdsmen, saying, "Bring to me here ten lambs without blemish

---

v. Literally "they have turned up their noses at"
w. Literally "male or female"
x. Sam 1:9–11, 26–28
y. Literally "Get down from here"
z. Literally "receive in the womb"

and without spot, and they will be for the Lord my God. And bring me twelve ₗyoungₗ[aa] calves, and they will be for the priests and for the assembly of the elders; and one hundred male goats for the whole people."

[4] And behold, Joachim came with his flocks, and Anna stood at the gate and saw Joachim coming, and ran and hung upon his neck, saying, "Now I know that the Lord God has blessed me exceedingly. For behold, the widow is no longer a widow, and the childless one ₗwill conceiveₗ."[ab] And Joachim rested the first day in his house.

[5.1] And on the next day he offered his gifts, saying to himself, "If the Lord God be merciful to me, the priest's leaf[ac] will ₗmake it plainₗ[ad] to me." And Joachim offered his gifts and looked earnestly upon the leaf of the priest when he went up to the altar of the Lord, and he saw no sin in himself. And Joachim said, "Now I know that the Lord has become merciful to me and has forgiven all my sins." And he went down from the temple of the Lord justified, and went to his house.

[2] And her months were fulfilled, and in the ninth month Anna gave birth. And she said to the midwife, "What have I borne?" And she said, "A female." And Anna said, "My soul is magnified this day," and she laid herself down. And when the days were fulfilled, Anna purified herself and ₗbegan to breastfeedₗ[ae] her child and called her name Mary.

[6.1] And day by day the child grew stronger. And when she was six months old, her mother stood her up on the ground to see if she would stand. And she walked seven steps and returned to her bosom. And she lifted her up, saying, "As the Lord my God lives, you will no longer walk on this ground, until I bring you into the temple of the Lord." And she made a sanctuary in her bedroom and did not allow anything common or unclean to pass

---

aa. Literally "tender"
ab. Literally "will receive in womb"
ac. Obscure. M. R. James offers "the plate *that is upon the forehead* of the priest"
ad. Literally "make it visible"
ae. Literally "gave her breast to"

through it. And she called for the undefiled daughters of the Hebrews, and they carried her here and there.

² And ₍the child had her first birthday₎,ᵃᶠ and Joachim made a great feast and called the priests and the scribes and the assembly of the elders and the whole people of Israel. And Joachim brought the child to the priests and they blessed her, saying, "O God of our fathers, bless this child and give her a name renowned forever among all generations." And all the people said, "So be it, so be it. Amen." And he brought her to the high priests and they blessed her, saying, "O God of the high places, look upon this child, and bless her with ₍the unsurpassable blessing₎."ᵃᵍ ³ And her mother took her up into the sanctuary of her bedchamber and ₍nursed her₎.ᵃʰ

And Anna made a song to the Lord God, saying:

> "I will sing a hymn to the Lord my God,
>   because he has visited me and taken the reproach of my
>   enemies away from me.
> And the Lord has given me the fruit of his righteousness,
>   single *and* abundant before him.
>
> Who will declare to the childrenᵃⁱ of Reuben
>   that Anna is breastfeeding?ᵃʲ
> Listen! You listen, twelve tribes of Israel,
>   that Anna is breastfeeding."

And she laid her to rest in the bedchamber of her sanctuary, and went forth and ministered to them. And when the feast was ended, they went down rejoicing and glorifying the God of Israel.

⁷·¹ And months passed by for the child, and the child became two years old. And Joachim said, "Let us bring her up to the temple of the Lord that we

---

af. Literally "it became the first year to the child"
ag. Literally "the ultimate blessing, which has no successor"
ah. Literally "gave her the breast"
ai. Or "sons"
aj. Gen 21:7

may pay the promise which we promised, lest the Lord ₗrequire it of usₗ[ak] and our gift become unacceptable." And Anna said, "Let us wait until the third year, so that the child may not long after her father or mother." And Joachim said, "Let us wait."[al]

² And the child became three years old. And Joachim said, "Call for the undefiled daughters of the Hebrews, and let them each take a lamp, and let them be burning, so that the child will not turn backward and her heart be taken captive away from the temple of the Lord." And they did so until they had gone up into the temple of the Lord.

And the priest received her and kissed her and blessed her and said, "The Lord has magnified your name among all generations. In you, at the end of days, the Lord will make his redemption visible to the children[am] of Israel." And he made her to sit upon the third step of the altar. And the Lord put grace upon her and she danced with her feet and all the house of Israel loved her.

8.1 And her parents came down marveling and praising the Lord God because the child ₗwas not rejectedₗ.[an]

And Mary was in the temple of the Lord, nurtured like a dove. And she received food from the hand of an angel.

² And when she was twelve years old, there was a council of the priests, saying, "Behold, Mary has become twelve years old in the temple of the Lord. What then shall we do with her, lest she defile the sanctuary of the Lord?" And they said to the high priest, "You stand over the altar of the Lord. Enter in and pray concerning her, and whatever the Lord will reveal to you, this we will also do."

---

ak. Literally "send unto us"
al. Sam 1:21–23
am. Or "sons"
an. Literally "was not turned away backward"

3 And the high priest took the robe with the twelve bells[ao] and went in unto the holy of holies and prayed concerning her. And behold, an angel of the Lord appeared, saying unto him, "Zacharias, Zacharias, go out and assemble those of the people who are widowers, and let them each bring a rod, and to whomever the Lord shall show a sign, she will be his wife." And the heralds went out across all the country around Judea, and the trumpet of the Lord sounded, and everyone ran *out to meet them.*

9.1 And Joseph threw down his axe and ran to meet them. And when they were gathered together they went to the high priest, taking their rods. And taking all of the rods, he went into the temple and prayed. And when he had finished the prayer, he took the rods and went out and gave them back to them, and there was no sign upon them. But Joseph received the last rod, and behold, a dove came out of the rod and flew upon Joseph's head. And the priest said to Joseph, "It has fallen to you to take the virgin of the Lord and keep her for yourself." 2 And Joseph refused, saying, "I have sons, and I am an old man, but she is a girl; lest I became a laughingstock to the children[ap] of Israel." And the priest said to Joseph, "Fear the Lord your God, and remember what God did to Dathan and Abiram and Korah, how the earth opened up and they were swallowed up because of their rebellion.[aq] And now you be afraid, Joseph, lest it also happen in your house." And Joseph was afraid, and took her to keep her for himself. And Joseph said to Mary, "Behold, I have received you from the temple of the Lord: and now I leave you in my house, and I am going away to build my buildings, and I will come *back* to you. The Lord will watch over you."

10.1 Now there was a council of the priests, and they said, "Let us make a veil for the temple of the Lord." And the priest said, "Call to me undefiled virgins from the tribe of David." And the officers departed and sought and found seven virgins. And the priests remembered the child Mary, that she was of the tribe of David and was undefiled before God. And the officers went and brought her back. And they brought them into the temple of the

---

ao. Exod 28:33–35
ap. Or "sons"
aq. Num 16:1, 31–35

Lord, and the priest said, "Cast me lots, which *of you* shall weave the gold and the ₗwhiteₗ[ar] and the fine linen and the silk and the hyacinth,[as] and the scarlet and the true purple." And the lot of the true purple and the scarlet fell to Mary, and she took them and went to her house.

And at that time Zacharias ₗbecame unable to talk,ₗ[at au] and Samuel was in his place until the time when Zacharias spoke *again*. But Mary took the scarlet and began to spin it.

11.1 And she took the pitcher and went forth to fill it with water. And behold, *she heard* a voice saying, "Greetings, you who are highly favored! The Lord is with you; you are blessed among women." And she looked ₗall around,[av] to see from where this voice *came*. And frightened, she went into her house and set down the pitcher, and took the purple and sat down upon her seat and stretched it.[aw]

2 And behold, an angel of the Lord stood before her, saying, "Fear not, Mary, for you have found grace before the Master of all things, and you will conceive of his word." And she, when she heard it, questioned ₗin her mind,ₗ[ax] saying, "Will I myself conceive of the living God, and ₗgive birthₗ[ay] after the manner of all women?" And the angel of the Lord said, "Not so, Mary, for a power of the Lord will overshadow you. Therefore also the holy one that will be born of you will be called the Son of the Highest. And you will call his name Jesus, for he shall save his people from their sins." And Mary said, "Behold the slave of the Lord is before him. Let it be unto me according to your word."[az]

---

ar. Literally "undefiled"
as. Or "deep blue"
at. Literally "became silent"
au. Luke 1:18–23
av. Literally "about her upon the right hand and upon the left"
aw. Luke 1:28–29
ax. Literally "in herself"
ay. Literally "bring forth"
az. Luke 1:30–38

¹²·¹ And she made the purple and the scarlet and brought them to the priest. And the priest blessed her and said, "Mary, the Lord God has magnified your name, and you will be blessed among all generations of the earth." ² And Mary rejoiced and went away to Elizabeth her relative.ᵇᵃ And she knocked at the door. And Elizabeth, upon hearing *it*, cast down the scarlet and ran to the door and opened it, and upon seeing Mary she blessed her and said: "₁Why did this happen to me₁,ᵇᵇ that the mother of my Lord should come to me? For behold, the *child* in me leaped and blessed you." And Mary forgot the mysteries that Gabriel the archangel had told her, and she looked up into the sky and said, "Who am I, Lord, that all the generations of the earth do bless me?" ³ And she stayed with Elizabeth for three months, and ₁every day₁ᵇᶜ her womb grew.ᵇᵈ And Mary was afraid and departed for her house and hid herself from the childrenᵇᵉ of Israel. Now she was sixteen years old when these mysteries came to pass.

¹³·¹ Now it was her sixth month, and behold, Joseph came from his building. And he entered into his house and found her ₁very pregnant₁,ᵇᶠ And he struck his face, and threw himself down upon the ground on sackcloth and wept bitterly, saying, "₁How can I possibly look₁ᵇᵍ upon the Lord my God? And what prayer will I make concerning this young woman? For I received her from the temple of the Lord my God a virgin, and I have not kept her safe. Who is he that trapped me? Who has done this evil in my own house and has defiled the virgin? Is not the story of Adam repeated in me? For as at the hour of his giving thanks the serpent came and found Eve alone and deceived her, so has it fallen to me also." ² And Joseph got up from off the sackcloth and called Mary and said to her, "O you who was cared for by God, why have you done this? You have forgotten the Lord your God. Why have you humbled your soul, you who were brought up in the holy of holies and received food at the hand of an angel?" ³ But she wept bitterly, saying, "I am pure and have not known a man." And Joseph said to her, "From where,

---

ba. Or "kinswoman"
bb. Literally "from where is this to me"
bc. Literally "day by day"
bd. Luke 1:39–45
be. Or "sons"
bf. Literally "great with child"
bg. Literally "with what countenance shall I look"

then, is that which is in your womb?" And she said, "As the Lord my God lives, I do not know from where it is come to me."

¹⁴·¹ And Joseph was exceeding fearful and left her alone and pondered what he should do with her. And Joseph said, "If I hide her sin, I will be found fighting against the law of the Lord, yet if I reveal her to the children[bh] of Israel, I fear because if that which is in her ⌊really is⌋[bi] the seed of an angel, then I will be found delivering up innocent blood to the judgment of death. What then shall I do? I will let her go from me secretly."[bj] And the night came upon him. ² And behold, an angel of the Lord appeared to him in a dream, saying, "Do not be afraid of this child, for that which is in her is of the Holy Spirit, and she will bear a son and you will call his name Jesus, for he will save his people from their sins." And Joseph got up from his sleep and glorified the God of Israel who had shown this favor to him, and he watched over her.[bk]

¹⁵·¹ Now Annas the scribe came to him and said to him, "Why did you not appear in our assembly?" And Joseph said to him, "I was weary with the journey, and I rested the first day." And Annas turned around and saw Mary ⌊very pregnant⌋.[bl] ² And he hastily went to the priest and said to him, "Joseph, ⌊the one you testified for⌋,[bm] has grievously sinned." And the priest said, "How so?" And he said, "The virgin whom he received from the temple of the Lord, he has defiled her, and ⌊secretly married her⌋,[bn] and has not declared it to the children[bo] of Israel." And the priest answered and said: "Has Joseph done this?" And Annas the scribe said, "Send officers, and you will find the virgin ⌊very pregnant⌋."[bp] And the officers went and found as he had said, and they brought her together with Joseph to the place of judgment. ³ And the priest said, "Mary, why have you done this, and why

---

bh. Or "sons"
bi. Literally "be"
bj. Matt 1:19
bk. Matt 1:20–25
bl. Literally "great with child"
bm. Literally "to whom you bore witness"
bn. Literally "stolen her marriage"
bo. Or "sons"
bp. Literally "great with child"

have you humbled your soul and forgotten the Lord your God, you who were nurtured in the holy of holies and who received food at the hand of an angel and who heard the hymns and danced before *the Lord*, why have you done this?"

But she wept bitterly, saying, "As the Lord my God lives, I am pure before him and have not known a man." 4 And the priest said to Joseph, "Why have you done this?" And Joseph said, "As the Lord my God lives, I am pure concerning her." And the priest said, "Do not bear false witness, but speak the truth. You have ₁secretly married her₁,[bq] and have not declared it to the children[br] of Israel, and have not bowed your head under the mighty hand that your seed should be blessed." And Joseph held his peace.

16.1 And the priest said, "Return the virgin whom you received from the temple of the Lord." And Joseph was full of weeping. And the priest said, "I will give you the water of the conviction of the Lord[bs] to drink, and it will make your sins visible before your eyes." 2 And taking *the water* the priest made Joseph drink and sent him into the hill country. And he returned whole. And the priest also made Mary drink and sent her into the hill country. And she returned whole. And all the people marveled, because sin was not revealed in them. 3 And the priest said, "If the Lord God has not made your sin visible, neither do I condemn you." And he let them go. And Joseph took Mary and departed to his house rejoicing, and glorifying the God of Israel.

17.1 Now there went out a decree from Augustus the king that all who were in Bethlehem of Judea should be registered *for a census*.[bt] And Joseph said, "I will register my sons, but this child, what shall I do? How shall I register her? As my wife? I am ashamed. Or as my daughter? But all the children[bu] of Israel know that she is not my daughter. This day of the Lord will happen as the Lord desires." 2 And he saddled the donkey, and set her upon it, and

---

bq. Literally "stolen her marriage"
br. Or "sons"
bs. Num 5:11–31
bt. Luke 2:1–3
bu. Or "sons"

his son led it and Joseph followed after. And they came within three miles *of Bethlehem*, and Joseph turned around and saw her sad and said to himself, "Perhaps that which is within her distresses her." And again Joseph turned around and saw her laughing, and said to her, "Mary, ₁why is it₁ᵇᵛ that I see your expression ₁at one time happy₁ᵇʷ and ₁at another time sad₁?"ᵇˣ And Mary said to Joseph, "Because I see two peoples with my eyes, the one weeping and mourning and the other rejoicing and exulting."

³ And they came ₁to the halfway point₁,ᵇʸ and Mary said to him, "Take me down from the donkey, for that which is within me presses hard to come out." And he took her down from the donkey and said to her, "Where can I take you to hide your shame? For the place is desert."ᵇᶻ

18.1 And he found a cave there and brought her in, and set his sons beside her. And he went out and looked for a Hebrew midwife in the country of Bethlehem.

² Now I, Joseph,ᶜᵃ was walking, yet I did not walk. And I looked up to the air and saw that the air was astonished. And I looked up to the vault of heaven and saw it standing still, and the birds of the sky at rest. And I looked upon the earth and saw a dish laid out, and workmen lying *by it*, and their hands were in the dish. And those who were chewing did not chew, and those who were lifting *food* did not lift *it*, and those who put it to their mouth had not put it there. And behold, there were sheep being driven, and they did not go forward but stood still; and the shepherd lifted his hand to strike them with his staff, yet his hand remained up. And I looked upon the stream of the river and saw the mouths of the goats upon *the water*, yet they did not drink. And ₁suddenly₁ᶜᵇ all things were restored to their course.

---

bv. Literally "what to you is this"
bw. Literally "once laughing"
bx. Literally "once sad"
by. Literally "the middle of the way"
bz. Or "a wilderness"
ca. The text has Joseph in the first person.
cb. Literally "in a moment"

^{19.1} And behold, a woman was coming down from the hill country, and she said to me, "Man, where are you going?" And I said, "I am looking for a Hebrew midwife." And she answered and said to me, "Are you from Israel?" And I said to her, "Yes." And she said, "And who is she who ₗgives birth₁^{cc} in the cave?" And I said, "She who is betrothed to me." And she said to me, "Is she not your wife?" And I said to her, "It is Mary who was brought up in the temple of the Lord. And I received her to wife by lot, and she is not my wife, but she has conceived by the Holy Spirit." And the midwife said to him, "Is this the truth?" And Joseph said to her, "Come and see." And the midwife went with him.

² And they stood in the ₗentrance₁^{cd} of the cave. And behold, a bright cloud overshadowed the cave. And the midwife said,

> "My soul is magnified this day,
>> because my eyes have seen marvelous things:
>> because salvation has been born to Israel."

And immediately the cloud withdrew itself out of the cave, and a great light appeared in the cave so that our eyes could not endure it. And little by little that light withdrew itself until the young child appeared. And it went and ₗbegan to nurse from₁^{ce} the breast of its mother Mary.

And the midwife cried out and said, "This day is great to me, in that I have seen this new sight."^{cf} ³ And the midwife went out of the cave and Salome met her. And she said to her, "Salome, Salome, I have a new sight^{cg} to tell you: A virgin ₗhas given birth₁,^{ch} which is apart from her own nature." And Salome said, "As the Lord my God lives, if I do not put in my finger and prove her nature^{ci} I will not believe that a virgin ₗhas given birth₁."^{cj}

---

cc. Literally "brings forth"
cd. Literally "place"
ce. Literally "took"
cf. Or "wonder"
cg. Or "wonder"
ch. Literally "has brought forth"
ci. John 20:24–29
cj. Literally "has brought forth"

20.1 And the midwife went in and said to Mary, "Position yourself, for no small contention has arisen concerning you." And Salome put her finger into her ₁vagina₁^{ck} and cried out and said, "Woe for my iniquity and my unbelief, because I have tested the living God, and behold, my hand, burned by fire, falls off of me!" **2** And she bowed her knees to the Lord, saying, "O God of my ancestors,^{cl} remember that I am the seed of Abraham and Isaac and Jacob. Do not make me a public example for the children^{cm} of Israel, but restore me to the poor, for you know, Master, that in your name I administered my treatments, and received my livelihood^{cn} from you." **3** And behold, an angel of the Lord appeared, saying unto her, "Salome, Salome, the Lord has heard you. Bring your hand to the young child and pick him up, and there will be salvation and joy for you." **4** And Salome came near and picked him up, saying, "I will worship him, for a great king has been born to Israel." And behold, immediately Salome was healed. And she went out of the cave justified. And behold, a voice saying, "Salome, Salome, tell no one of the wonders that you have seen, until the child enters into Jerusalem."

21.1 And behold, Joseph prepared to go into Judea. And there was a great uproar in Bethlehem of Judea; for wise men came, saying, "Where is he who is born king of the Jews? For we have seen his star in the east and have come to worship him."^{co} **2** And when Herod heard it he was troubled and sent assistants to the wise men. And he sent for the high priests and questioned them, saying, "How is it written concerning the Christ, where he is born?" They said to him, "In Bethlehem of Judea, for so it is written." And he let them go. And he questioned the wise men, saying to them, "What sign did you see concerning the king who has been born?" And the wise men said, "We saw an incredibly great star shining among these stars, and dimming them so that the *normal* stars ₁disappeared₁.^{cp} And so we knew that a king was born in Israel, and we came to worship him." And Herod said, "Go and look for him, and if you find him, tell me, that I may also

---

ck. Literally "nature," compare BDAG φύσις 2
cl. Or "fathers"
cm. Or "sons"
cn. Or "wages"
co. Matt 2:1–12
cp. Literally "did not appear"

come and worship him." ³ And the wise men went out. And behold, the star that they saw in the east went before them until they entered into the cave. And it remained^{cq} over the ₗentrance₎^{cr} of the cave. And the wise men saw the young child with Mary his mother. And they took gifts out of their bags:^{cs} gold and frankincense and myrrh.^{ct} ⁴ And being warned by the angel that they should not enter into Judea, they went into their own country by another way.

²²·¹ But when Herod thought that he had been tricked^{cu} by the wise men, ₗhis anger was kindled₎^{cv} and he sent murderers, saying to them, "The infants, two years and under: kill *them*."^{cw} ² And when Mary heard that the infants were being killed, being fearful, she took the young child and wrapped him in swaddling clothes and laid him in a manger for cattle.^{cx}

³ But Elizabeth, when she heard that they were looking for John, took him and went up into the hill country and looked around *to see* where she could hide him. And there was no hiding place. And groaning, Elizabeth said with a loud voice, "Mountain of God, receive a mother with *her* child." For Elizabeth was not able to go up *the mountain*. And immediately the mountain split in two and took her in. And it was shining a light on them, for an angel of the Lord was with them, keeping watch over them.

²³·¹ Now Herod sought for John, and sent officers to Zacharias, saying, "Where have you hidden your son?" And he answered, saying to them, "I am a minister of God and attend continually upon the temple of the Lord. I do not know where my son is." ² And the assistants departed and told Herod all these things. And ₗwith growing anger₎^{cy} Herod said, "His son is about to be king over Israel." And he sent to him again, saying, "Tell the truth:

---

cq. Or "stood"
cr. Literally "head"
cs. Or "packs" or "baggage"
ct. Matt 2:11
cu. Or "duped"
cv. Literally "he became angry"
cw. Matt 2:16–18
cx. Luke 2:7
cy. Literally "being angry"

where is your son? For you know that your blood is under my hand." And the assistants departed and told him all these things. ³ And Zacharias said, "I am a martyr of God[cz] if you shed my blood, for the Lord shall receive my spirit, because you will shed innocent blood in the forecourt of the temple of the Lord."[da]

And when the day was dawning, Zacharias was slain. And the children[db] of Israel did not know that he was slain.

²⁴·¹ But the priests came out at the hour of the greeting, and the blessing of Zacharias did not meet them, ₍as it usually did₎.[dc] And the priests stood waiting for Zacharias, to greet him with a prayer, and to glorify the Most High. ² Upon *his* delay *in coming*, they were all afraid. And summoning courage,[dd] one of them entered in, and he saw congealed blood by the altar and *heard* a voice saying, "Zacharias has been murdered, and his blood will not be wiped away until his avenger comes." And upon hearing the word he was afraid, and went out and reported to the priests. ³ And summoning *their* courage[de] they went in and saw what had happened. And the panels of the temple cried out, and they tore apart *their clothes* from the top to the bottom. And they did not find his body, but they found his blood had turned to stone. And ₍in a state of fear₎[df] they went out and told all the people that Zacharias had been murdered. And all the tribes of the people heard, and they mourned for him and lamented him three days and three nights. ⁴ Now after the three days the priests took counsel whom they should appoint in his place, and the lot fell upon Simeon, for it was Simeon who was warned by the Holy Spirit that he would not see death until he should see the Christ in the flesh.[dg]

---

cz. Or "God's witness"
da. Matt 23:35; Luke 11:51
db. Or "sons"
dc. Literally "according to custom"
dd. Or "became bold"
de. Or "became bold"
df. Literally "being afraid"
dg. Luke 2:25–35

²⁵·¹ Now I, James, who wrote this history in Jerusalem, when a disturbance arose, when Herod died, withdrew myself into the wilderness until the disturbance ceased in Jerusalem, glorifying the Master, God, who gave me the gift and the wisdom to write this history.

² And grace will be with those who fear our Lord Jesus Christ: to whom be glory ₍forever and ever₎.ᵈʰ Amen.

SELECT BIBLIOGRAPHY

Ehrman, Bart D., and Zlatko Pleše. *The Apocryphal Gospels: Texts and Translations*. Oxford: Oxford University Press, 2010.

James, M. R. *The Apocryphal New Testament*. Oxford: Clarendon, 1924.

Porter, Stanley E. "Early Apocryphal Gospels and the New Testament Text." Pages 350–70 in *The Early Text of the New Testament*. Edited by Charles E. Hill and Michael J. Kruger. Oxford: Oxford University Press, 2012.

Strycker, E. de. *La forme la plus ancienne du Protévangile de Jacques*. Brussels: Société des Bollandistes, 1961.

Tischendorf, C. von. *Evangelia Apocrypha*. 2nd ed. Leipzig: Mendelssohn, 1876.

Vorster, Willem S. "James, Protevangelium of." ABD 3:629–32.

---

dh. Literally "into the ages of the ages"

— The Infancy Gospel of Thomas

INTRODUCTION

The *Infancy Gospel of Thomas* (*Inf. Gos. Thom.*) is a collection of stories, likely originating from an oral tradition, about Jesus between the ages of 5 and 12.[a] The stories are fantastic, portraying the boy Jesus as a sometimes spiteful and sometimes compassionate miracle worker. These stories appear to fill the gap in the Gospel narratives between Jesus' birth and early years (Matt 2; Luke 2:1–40) and Jesus in the temple at 12 years old (Luke 2:41–52).[b] Many of the episodes directly or indirectly foreshadow events in Jesus' adulthood recorded in the canonical Gospels.

The textual evidence exists in a few different recensions in 13 different language editions;[c] this complicates the process of creating a true critical edition and makes it difficult to establish the most ancient version.[d]

The text is thought to have originated in the second century,[e] although the earliest available material is from the fifth and sixth centuries in Syriac and Latin.[f] Tischendorf published two different recensions of the Greek text in his edition. What is known as "Recension A"[g] is based on 15th and 16th century manuscripts; "Recension B"[h] is shorter and based on a different

---

a. Paul Allan Mirecki, "Thomas, The Infancy Gospel of," *ABD* 6:540.
b. Ibid., 542.
c. Ibid., 540.
d. Bart D. Ehrman and Zlatko Pleše, *The Apocryphal Gospels: Texts and Translations* (Oxford: Oxford University Press, 2010), 4.
e. Oscar Cullmann, "The Infancy Story of Thomas," in *New Testament Apocrypha*, rev. ed., ed. Wilhelm Schneemelcher, trans. R. McL. Wilson (Louisville: Westminster John Knox, 1991), 1:439.
f. Ibid., 1:440–41; Ehrman and Pleše, *The Apocryphal Gospels*, 3.
g. C. von Tischendorf, *Evangelia Apocrypha*, 2nd ed. (Leipzig: Mendelssohn, 1876), 140–57.
h. Ibid., 158–163.

14th/15th century manuscript.[i] Most English translations of the Greek *Inf. Gos. Thom.* use Tischendorf's Recension A as their basis.[j]

CONTENT

Tischendorf's Recension A of *Inf. Gos. Thom.* consists of 19 chapters[k] with material in a roughly sequential order.

§1 is a prologue with "Thomas the Israelite" introducing the material, speaking in the first person.

§2 has a 5-year-old Jesus, with his words alone, miraculously gathering and purifying water at the ford of a stream. He also made 12 clay sparrows. However, he does this on a Sabbath, and someone reports it to his father, Joseph.

§3 opens with the son of Annas the scribe disturbing the waters that Jesus had gathered together. Jesus, perturbed, strikes the boy lame.

§4 begins a new episode, with another boy accidentally bumping into the boy Jesus. Jesus responds by striking the boy dead.

§5 Joseph admonishes Jesus for this action, and Jesus does not apologize. Instead, the boy Jesus blinds those who accused Him.

§6 begins an episode with a teacher named Zacchaeus who hopes to teach Jesus to read and write. Instead, Jesus confounds Zacchaeus with questions about the nature of the letter alpha.

§7 records Zacchaeus' frustration and despair at his failure in educating Jesus.

§8 continues the episode, with Jesus exhorting Zacchaeus and then, when he stops speaking, "all those who had fallen under his curse, they were immediately restored."

§9 records an episode with the boy Jesus' friend, Zenon, falling from a window and dying. Jesus is accused of pushing his friend; in response Jesus raises Zenon from the dead to confirm that he was not responsible for Zenon's death.

---

i. Cullmann, "The Infancy Story of Thomas," 1:439–440; Ehrman and Pleše, *The Apocryphal Gospels*, 7.

j. Cullmann, "The Infancy Story of Thomas," 1:443, as well as M. R. James, *The Apocryphal New Testament* (Oxford: Clarendon, 1924), 49.

k. Chapter breaks are modern.

§10 is another episode of healing. This time Jesus heals a man who wounded his foot with an axe.

§11 has a 6-year-old Jesus fetching water for his mother. The pitcher breaks in the crowd, but Jesus takes his cloak, fills it with water, and brings it home to his mother.

§12 tells of an episode with Jesus and Joseph sowing grain. Jesus sows one seed, and it yields more than 100 measures of grain, feeding the family and all the poor in the village.

§13 has Jesus helping Joseph build a bed by stretching a piece of wood that is too short.

§14 has Joseph again seeking a teacher for Jesus. This teacher, after Jesus' provocation, strikes Jesus on the head. Jesus responds by cursing the teacher and striking him down.

§15 has another teacher, a "true friend of Joseph," wanting to teach Jesus. This teacher respects Jesus, and in response Jesus heals the previous teacher.

§16 has Jesus and his older brother James gathering wood. A snake bites James' hand, and Jesus heals him by breathing on the wound.

§17 has Jesus raising a baby from the dead.

§18 has Jesus raising a construction worker from the dead.

§19 retells the story of Jesus at the Jerusalem temple during Passover (cf. Luke 2:41–52).

TRANSLATION

The translation is a reworking of M. R. James' translation,[l] heavily edited in consultation with Tischendorf's Recension A.[m]

The stories of Thomas the Israelite, the Philosopher, concerning the works of the childhood of the Lord.

1.1 I, Thomas the Israelite, report to you, all the brothers who are of the Gentiles, to make known to you the works of the childhood and greatness

---

l. James, *The Apocryphal New Testament*, 49–55.
m. Tischendorf, *Evangelia Apocrypha*, 140–157.

of our Lord Jesus Christ, all that he did when he was born in our land, the beginning of which is as follows.

2.1 This child Jesus, being five years old, was playing at the ford of a stream. And he gathered together the waters that flowed into pools, and immediately ₁purified them₁;[n] by his word alone he commanded them. ² And upon making soft clay, he fashioned twelve sparrows from it. And it was the Sabbath when he did these things. And there were also many other little children playing with him.

³ And a certain Jew, upon seeing what Jesus did, playing on the Sabbath day, departed at once and told his father Joseph, "Behold, your child is at the stream, and upon taking clay he made twelve little birds, and has desecrated the Sabbath." ⁴ And Joseph, upon coming to the place and seeing, cried out to him, saying, "Why do you do these things on the Sabbath, which it is not lawful to do?" But Jesus clapped his hands together and cried out to the sparrows and said to them, "Go!" And the sparrows took their flight and went away chirping. ⁵ And upon seeing it, the Jews were amazed. Departing, they told their superiors what they had seen Jesus do.

3.1 But the son of Annas the scribe was standing there with Joseph; and he took a willow branch and dispersed the waters that Jesus had gathered together. ² And Jesus, upon seeing what happened, was indignant and said to him, "You unjust, ungodly dimwit; what harm did the pools and the waters do to you? Behold, now you will also be withered like a tree, and will not bear leaves or root or fruit." ³ And immediately that child was completely withered up, but Jesus departed and went to Joseph's house. But the parents of the withered one took him up, mourning his youth, and brought him to Joseph, and accused him because "you have such a child, who does such things."

4.1 Then he again went through the village, and a child ran and bumped against his shoulder. And Jesus was irritated and said to him, "You will not continue along your way." And at once he fell down and died. But upon

---

n. Literally "made them clean"

seeing what happened, some said, "Where was this child born, because his every word is an accomplished work?" [2] And the parents of the dead child came to Joseph. They blamed *him*, saying, "You who have such a child cannot live with us in the village. Or teach him to bless and not to curse,[o] for he kills our children!"

[5.1] And Joseph called the child and privately admonished him, saying, "Why do you do such things, so that these people suffer and hate us and persecute us?" But Jesus said, "I know that your words, these words, are not yours. Nevertheless I will stay silent for your sake. But those others will bear their punishment." And immediately those who accused him were made blind. [2] And those who saw *it* were greatly afraid and perplexed, and said about him that every word that he spoke, whether it was good or bad, was a work, and became a wondrous *thing*. And when they saw what Jesus had done, Joseph, getting up, took his ear and pulled it hard. [3] And the child was irritated and said to him, "It is enough for you to seek and not to find, and you have acted especially unwisely. Do you not know that I am yours? Do not grieve me."

[6.1] Now a certain teacher, Zacchaeus by name, stood there, and he heard in part when Jesus said these things to his father, and ⌊he was astounded⌋[p] that, being a child, he uttered such things. [2] And after a few days he approached Joseph and said unto him, "You have a wise child, and he has understanding. Come, hand him over to me so that he may learn letters. And I will teach him with the letters all knowledge, and to greet all the elders and honor them as grandfathers and fathers, and love his contemporaries." [3] And he told him all the letters from the alpha to the omega clearly, with much questioning. But looking upon Zacchaeus the teacher, he said to him, "You do not know the alpha according to its nature; how can you teach others the beta? You hypocrite! First, if you know *it*, teach the alpha, and then we will believe you regarding the beta." Then he began to ⌊closely question⌋[q] the teacher concerning the first letter, and he was not able to answer him.

---

o. Rom 12:14
p. Literally "he wondered exceedingly"
q. Literally "confound the mouth of"

[4] And when many others ₍were within earshot₎,[r] the child said to Zacchaeus, "Listen, teacher, to the succession of the first letter and pay attention to this, how it has lines and a middle mark that you can see, common to both, going apart, coming together, raised up high but again coming down, three marks alike in kind. You have the rules of the alpha."[s]

7.1 Now when Zacchaeus the teacher heard the many and varied allegories of the first letter spoken by the child, he was perplexed at his answer and his instruction being so great, and said to those who were there, "Woe is me, wretch that I am, I am confounded. I have brought shame to myself by bringing on this child. [2] So take him away, I implore you, brother Joseph! I cannot endure the severity of his look; I cannot understand a single word. This child is not born *of this earth*. This one can even tame fire. Perhaps this one was born before the world was made. What ₍uterus₎[t] bore this one, what womb nurtured this one? ₍I have no idea₎.[u] Woe is me, friend. He confuses me; I cannot follow his understanding. I have deceived myself ₍three times over₎.[v] I strove to get myself a disciple and I am found to have a teacher. [3] Friends, I consider my shame. For being an old man, I have been overcome by a child; and I am ready to faint and to die because of the boy, for at this hour I am not able to look him in the face. And when everyone says that I have been overcome by a little child, what do I have to say? And what can I say about the rules of the first letter he told me? I am ignorant, friends, for I know neither beginning nor end of it.[w] [4] For this very reason, I implore you, brother Joseph, take him away to your house. He has some sort of greatness, whether god or angel or what I should call him, I do not know."

8.1 And as the Jews were counseling Zacchaeus, the child laughed greatly and said, "Now let those who are yours[x] bear fruit and let the blind in heart see. I have come from above so that I may curse them, and call them to the

---

r. Literally "were listening"
s. Here Jesus explains the order of the pen strokes that make an alpha. Similar sayings are also found in the writings of gnostics (see Irenaeus, *Haer.* 1.20.1)
t. Literally "stomach"
u. Literally "I do not know"
v. Literally "three times unhappy me"
w. Or "him"
x. Some versions have "who are barren"

things that are above, just as the one who sent me commanded for your sake." ² And when the child ₁stopped talking₁,ʸ all those who had fallen under his curse, they were immediately restored. And nobody after that dared to provoke him, lest he curse him, and he become crippled.

⁹·¹ Now after a few days Jesus was playing in the upper story of a particular house, and one of the children who played with him fell down from the house and died. And upon seeing *it*, the other children fled, and Jesus remained alone. ² And upon arriving, the parents of the dead child accused him that he had thrown him down. And Jesus said, "I did not throw him down." But they reviled him still. ³ Then Jesus jumped down from the roof and stood by the body of the child and cried with a loud voice and said, "Zenon!" (for so was his name called), "get up and tell me, did I throw you down?" And getting up at once, he said, "No, Lord, you did not throw me down, but you did raise me up!" And when they saw it they were amazed. And the parents of the child glorified God for the sign that had occurred, and worshiped Jesus.

¹⁰·¹ After a few days, a certain young man was splitting wood in the ₁neighborhood₁,ᶻ and the axe fell and split apart the sole of his foot, and ₁having lost a significant amount of blood₁ᵃᵃ he was at the point of death. ² And there was an uproar and ₁a crowd was forming₁,ᵃᵇ *and* the child Jesus also ran there. And forcing his way, he cut through the crowd and took hold of the foot of the young man who was injured, and immediately it was healed. And he said to the young man, "Now get up, split the wood, and remember me." But the crowd, upon seeing what had happened, worshiped the young child, saying, "Truly the spirit of God dwells in this young child."

¹¹·¹ Now when he was six years old, his mother sent him to draw water and carry it into the house, giving him a pitcher. But in the crowd, colliding *against another*, the pitcher was broken. ² But Jesus spread out the garment

---

y. Literally "stopped the word"
z. Literally "corner"
aa. Literally "becoming bloodless"
ab. Literally "running together"

ɪhe was wearing,ₗᵃᶜ filled it with water, and brought it to his mother. And his mother, upon seeing the sign that happened, kissed him; and she kept to herself the mysteries that she saw him do.ᵃᵈ

12.1 And again, in the time of sowing the child went out with his father to sow wheat in their land.ᵃᵉ And as his father sowed, the child Jesus also sowed one seed of wheat. 2 And upon reaping and threshing it, he made one hundred ₗmeasuresₗ.ᵃᶠᵃᵍ And calling all the poor of the village to the threshing-floor, he gave the wheat to them. And Joseph took the remainder of the wheat. And he was eight years old when he performed this sign.

13.1 Now his father was a carpenter, and at that time he made plows and yokes. And a bed was ordered by a certain rich man, that he should make it for him. But when one beam, that which is called the shifting one, was too short, he did not know what to do. The young child Jesus said to his father Joseph, "Lay down the two pieces of wood and make it even from the middle part." And Joseph did as the child said to him. And Jesus stood at the other end and took hold of the shorter beam and stretched it and made it equal with the other. And his father Joseph saw it and was astounded. And he hugged the child and kissed him, saying, "I am blessed that God has given me this child."

14.1 But Joseph, upon seeing the understanding of the child, and his age, that it was coming to the point of maturity, again thought to himself that ₗhe should not be illiterate,ₗᵃʰ and taking him he brought him to another teacher. And the teacher said to Joseph, "First I will teach him the Greek letters, and after that the Hebrew." For the teacher knew the skill of the child and was afraid of him. Nevertheless, upon writing the alphabet he practiced it many hours, and Jesus did not answer him. 2 And Jesus said to him, "If you are indeed a teacher, and if you know letters well, tell me

---

ac. Literally "which was upon him"
ad. Luke 2:19, 51
ae. Matt 13:3–8; Mark 4:3–8; Luke 8:5–8
af. Literally "cors." A cor measures between 10 and 12 bushels (BDAG χόρος, p. 560).
ag. Luke 16:7
ah. Literally "he should not be ignorant of letters"

the power of the alpha, and I will tell you the power of the beta." Upon being provoked, the teacher hit him on the head. And the child, hurting, cursed him, and immediately he fainted and fell to the ground on his face. ³ And the child returned to the house of Joseph: and Joseph was grieved and ordered his mother,[ai] "Do not let him out the door, because those who provoke him to anger die."

¹⁵·¹ And after some time yet another teacher[aj] who was a true friend of Joseph said to him, "Bring the child to me, to the school. Perhaps I may be able to teach him the letters by flattering him." And Joseph said, "If you have no fear, my brother, take him with you." And he took the child with him in fear and great trembling, but the child followed him gladly. ² And going with boldness into the school, he found a book laying upon the lectern.[ak] And taking it, he did not read the letters that were in it, but upon opening his mouth he spoke by the Holy Spirit, and taught the law to those who stood by. And a great crowd, coming together, stood there listening to him, and were in awe at the beauty of his teaching and the readiness of his words, that being an infant he spoke such things. ³ But upon hearing it, Joseph was afraid, and he ran to the school, wondering if this teacher[al] was also without skill. But the teacher[am] said to Joseph, "You should know, my brother, that I received the child as a disciple, but he is full of much grace and wisdom. And now I ask you, brother, take him to your house." ⁴ And when the child heard this, he immediately smiled[an] at him and said, "Since you have spoken rightly and testified rightly, for your sake the one who was smitten will be healed." And at once the other teacher was healed. And Joseph took the child and went to his house.

¹⁶·¹ And Joseph sent his son James to bundle wood and bring it *back* to his house. And the child Jesus also followed him. And as James was gathering firewood, a snake bit James' hand.[ao] ² And as he was laid out and dying, Jesus

---

ai. That is, the child's mother, Mary
aj. Or "guide"
ak. Or "reading desk"
al. Or "guide"
am. Or "guide"
an. Or "laughed"
ao. Acts 28:3–6

approached and breathed on the bite. And immediately the pain ceased, and the snake burst, and at once James became healthy.

17.1 And after these things, in the neighborhood of Joseph, an infant became sick and died,[ap] and his mother wept exceedingly. And Jesus heard that there was great mourning and trouble, and he ran *there* quickly. And he found the child dead, and he touched his breast and said, "I say to you, baby, do not die, but live and be with your mother." And looking up at once, it laughed. And he said to the woman, "Take him up and give him milk, and remember me." 2 And upon seeing *it*, the crowd standing by was amazed, and said, "Truly this child is either a god or an angel of God; for every word of his is a completed work." And Jesus departed from there, even playing with other children.

18.1 And after some time ₎a house was being built₎.[aq] And *there was* a great uproar, and Jesus stood up and went there. And upon seeing a man lying dead, he took hold of his hand and said, "I say to you, man, get up and do your work."[ar] And immediately he got up and worshiped him. 2 And upon seeing *it*, the crowd was amazed, and said, "This child is from heaven, for he has saved many souls from death, and ₎is able to save₎[as] them all his whole life."

19.1 And when he was twelve years old, his parents went according to the custom to Jerusalem to the feast of the Passover with their caravan.[at] And after the Passover they returned to their house. And as they returned, the child Jesus went back to Jerusalem, but his parents supposed that he was in their caravan. 2 And after traveling a day's journey, they sought him among their relatives. And upon not finding him, they were distressed, and returned again to the city looking for him. And after the third day they found him in the temple sitting in the midst of the teachers, both listening to them and asking *questions*. And they all paid attention to him, and were

---

ap. Luke 7:11–17
aq. Literally "a house became"
ar. Luke 7:14; Mark 5:41
as. Literally "he has to save"
at. A group of travelers

amazed how as yet a child he put to silence the elders and teachers of the people, explaining ₍the major tenets₎[au] of the law and the parables of the prophets. ³ And coming close, his mother Mary said to him, "Why have you done this to us, child? Behold, in distress we have been looking for you!" And Jesus said to them, "Why did you look for me? Do you not know that I must be in my Father's house?"[av] ⁴ But the scribes and Pharisees said, "Are you the mother of this child?" And she said, "I am." And they said to her, "You are blessed among women, because God has blessed the fruit of your womb.[aw] For such glory and such excellence and wisdom we have neither seen nor heard at any time."

⁵ And Jesus got up and followed his mother and was subject[ax] to his parents. But his mother ₍treasured₎[ay] all that happened. And Jesus increased in wisdom and stature and grace. To him be glory ₍forever and ever₎,[az] Amen.

SELECT BIBLIOGRAPHY

Cullmann, Oscar. "The Infancy Story of Thomas." Pages 439–52 in Vol. 1 of *New Testament Apocrypha*. Rev. ed. Edited by Wilhelm Schneemelcher. Translated by R. McL. Wilson. 2 vols. Louisville: Westminster John Knox, 1991.

Ehrman, Bart D., and Zlatko Pleše. *The Apocryphal Gospels: Texts and Translations*. Oxford: Oxford University Press, 2010.

James, M. R. *The Apocryphal New Testament*. Oxford: Clarendon, 1924.

Mirecki, Paul Allan. "Thomas, The Infancy Gospel of." *ABD* 6:540–44.

Tischendorf, C. von. *Evangelia Apocrypha*. 2nd ed. Leipzig: Mendelssohn, 1876.

---

au. Literally "the head"
av. Luke 2:41–52
aw. Luke 1:42
ax. Or "obedient"
ay. Literally "kept"
az. Literally "into the ages of the ages"

— The Gospel of Peter

INTRODUCTION

While discussion of a gospel written in Peter's name dates at least to the third century,[a] its contents were unknown until the late 19th century. What is now known of the *Gospel of Peter* (*Gos. Pet.*) comes from one section (nine pages) of parchment codex known as P.Cair. 10759. The codex is variously dated, from "5th-6th century"[b] to "late 6th century"[c] to "seventh or eighth century"[d] to "latter half of the eighth century."[e] This codex, found in a cemetery in Ahkmîm, Egypt in 1886-87,[f] also contains a portion of the *Apocalypse of Peter* and a portion of *1 Enoch*.[g]

Two fragments from Oxyrhynchus, P.Oxy. 2949 and P.Oxy. 4009, are commonly associated with *Gos. Pet.* The former, dated to the late second or early third century,[h] appears to share an episode (*Gos. Pet.* 2.3-5) with P.Cair. 10759, as well as a unique description of Joseph of Arimathea, "Joseph, the friend of Pilate."[i] The latter, dated to the second century,[j] is more tenta-

a. Bart D. Ehrman and Zlatko Pleše, *The Apocryphal Gospels: Texts and Translations* (Oxford: Oxford University Press, 2010), 371.

b. Bernard P. Grenfell and Arthur S. Hunt, eds., *Catalogue Général des Antiquitiés Égyptiennes du Musée du Caire, Nos. 10001-10869: Greek Papyri* (Oxford: Oxford University Press, 1903), 98.

c. Andrew Bernhard, *Other Early Christian Gospels: A Critical Edition of the Surviving Greek Manuscripts* (London: T&T Clark, 2007), 51.

d. H. B. Swete, *The Akhmîm Fragment of the Apocryphal Gospel of Peter* (London: Macmillan, 1893), xlvi.

e. Paul Allan Mirecki, "Peter, Gospel of," *ABD* 5:279.

f. Bernhard, *Other Early Christian Gospels*, 49.

g. Grenfell and Hunt, *Greek Papyri*, 98.

h. Bernhard, *Other Early Christian Gospels*, 52.

i. Ibid., 49.

j. Ibid., 51.

tive. It relates a relatively common agraphon also found in 2 *Clem.* 5.2–4,[k] a discussion between Jesus and Peter about sheep and wolves. Unlike 2 *Clement*, however, P.Oxy. 4009 witnesses the discussion from the perspective of Peter. Thus, P.Oxy. 4009 is thought to possibly witness to an unknown portion of *Gos. Pet.*

There are two other fragments that have sometimes been associated with *Gos. Pet.*, although their identification rests on conjecture. One of these fragments, P.Oxy. 1224,[l] also contains an account of Jesus from a first-person perspective. Some have suggested the perspective could be that of Peter,[m] but unlike P.Oxy. 4009, there are no alternate versions to add support to this idea.

The second possible fragment, P.Vindob. G 2325,[n] includes the name of Peter in red ink as a *nomina sacra*. Lührmann has suggested a reconstruction of one portion to a first-person pronoun, which would shift the speaker to Peter and thus provide support for considering it to be a fragment of *Gos. Pet.*[o]

Because of the tentative nature of the connections between both of these fragments and *Gos. Pet.*, both P.Oxy. 1224 and P.Vindob. G 2325 are discussed in the introduction to fragments.

Numbering Systems

Several editions of *Gos. Pet.* with different numbering systems have been published in the past 100 years. Harnack's edition[p] segmented the text into 14 sections; Swete's edition has 12 sections;[q] other editions number the sentences from 1 to 60.[r] Convention has combined the 14-section system and the 60-sentence system, citing both to allow portability of references

---

k. See discussion on 2 *Clement* 5.2–4 in the introduction to the agrapha.

l. See discussion on P.Oxy. 1224 in the section on fragments.

m. Bernhard, *Other Early Christian Gospels*, 50.

n. See discussion on P.Vindob. G 2325 in the section on fragments.

o. D. Lührmann and E. Schlarb, *Fragmente apokryph gewordener Evangelien in Griechischer und lateinischer Sprache*, Marburger theologische Studien 59 (Marburg: N. G. Elwert, 2000), 74.

p. A. Harnack, *Bruchstücke des Evangeliums und der Apokalypse des Petrus* (Leipzig: J. C. Hinrichs'sche Buchhandlung, 1893).

q. Swete, *The Akhmîm Fragment of the Apocryphal Gospel of Peter.* Swete's §9 = Harnack's §9–10; S§10 = H§11; S§11 = H§12–13; S§12 = H§14.

r. J. A. Robinson, "The Gospel according to Peter," in *The Gospel According to Peter and the Revelation of Peter: Two Lectures on the Newly Recovered Fragments Together with the Greek Texts*, ed. M. R. James and J. A. Robinson (London: C. J. Clay, 1892).

across editions. So a reference to *Gos. Pet.* 2.3–5 indicates §2 (of the 14-section system) and sentences 3–5 of the 60-sentence system.

CONTENT

The content of the *Gos. Pet.*[s] is similar to the four canonical Gospels. It contains an account of the judgment, punishment, crucifixion, and resurrection of Jesus. It uses some details known from the Gospels, omits others, and adds its own.[t] Because of this, it is generally accepted that *Gos. Pet.* has a relationship with the Gospels, but the nature of this relationship is disputed. Ehrman and Pleše offer four possibilities:[u]

1. *Gos. Pet.* is a later conglomeration of the earlier canonical Gospels with some legendary material added.

2. *Gos. Pet.* is the product of an author who was familiar with the earlier canonical Gospels but misremembered some details in writing his own gospel. Ehrman and Pleše associate this view with Hans-Josef Klauck.

3. *Gos. Pet.* is the product of an author familiar with oral traditions of Jesus, but writing independently. Ehrman and Pleše associate this view with Ehrman.

4. *Gos. Pet.* is the product of an author with a source that predated the canonical Gospels; this source also better preserved the material and so represents an earlier form of the accounts of Jesus' death and resurrection. Ehrman and Pleše associate this view with John Dominic Crossan.

Of these four possibilities, some combination of two and three is the likeliest solution.

---

s. When *Gos. Pet.* is mentioned generically, P.Cair. 10759 is meant.
t. Swete, *The Akhmîm Fragment*, xiii—xviii.
u. Ehrman and Pleše, *The Apocryphal Gospels*, 375.

DOCETISM

Church fathers from as early as the third century knew of a gospel attributed to Peter. Origen (*Comm. Matt.* 10.17) and Eusebius (*Eccl. Hist.* 3.3.2; 3.25.6) both mention it, although Eusebius lists it among disavowed writings because of its popularity among docetists.[v] Docetism, (from δοκέω *dokeō*, "to seem," or "to appear as") is the label given to an early church heresy that taught that Jesus seemed to be human, but was in fact spirit. Thus, according to docetists, he only appeared to suffer and die.

Eusebius reports of Serapion, bishop of Antioch, who approved the use of *Gos. Pet.*, apparently without having read it. Later, when Serapion learned that docetists were using it, he wrote a tract about its problematic material and forbade its use.[w]

DISTINCTIVES

The text of *Gos. Pet.* contains material found nowhere else. Two of the most notable examples are the request for Jesus' body (*Gos. Pet.* 2.3–5; P.Oxy. 2949) and the walking, talking cross (*Gos. Pet.* 10.38–42).

Gospel of Peter 2.3–5 is an account of Joseph of Arimathea's request for Jesus' body, but it differs from the canonical accounts (Matt 27:58; Mark 15:43–45; Luke 23:50–53; John 19:38). First, it differs in how it describes Joseph. Instead of being associated with Arimathea or the council, Joseph is "a friend of Pilate" in both P.Cair. 10759 and P.Oxy. 2949. These are the only known instances of this descriptor.

Second, the account differs in the timing of Joseph's request for Jesus' body. In the canonical accounts, the request is made after Jesus died. In *Gos. Pet.*, the request is made before the crucifixion, when he realized "they were about to crucify [Jesus]."

Third, the account of *Gos. Pet.* differs in detail. The canonical accounts simply record Pilate releasing the body to Joseph. The *Gos. Pet.*, however, has Pilate asking Herod for the body before the crucifixion occurs. There is a discussion between Pilate and Herod, where the Old Testament law (Deut 21:23) is recalled and used as justification to release the body to Joseph, to ensure proper burial.

---

v. Ibid., 371.
w. Ibid., 371–72.

The most distinctive episode in *Gos. Pet.* is the episode of giant angels and the walking, talking cross found in *Gos. Pet.* 10.38–42. This takes place "on the night when the Lord's Day was drawing on, as the soldiers kept guard two by two in a watch" (*Gos. Pet.* 9.35), before Mary and the other women arrive at the tomb:

> 10.38 The soldiers, therefore, when they saw it, awakened the centurion and the elders (for they were also there keeping watch); 39 and as they told the things that they had seen, again they saw three men coming from the tomb, two of them supporting the other, and a cross following them. 40 And the head of the two reached to heaven, but that of him who was led by them overpassed the heavens. 41 And they heard a voice from the heavens, saying, "You preached to the ones who are sleeping?" 42 And a response was heard from the cross, "Yes."

The picture is of two angels whose heads "reached to heaven" supporting a third person, Jesus, who is larger than even the angels, and a cross following behind them. The function of the walking, talking cross is hard to understand.

One recent proposal by Mark Goodacre[x] suggests an emendation of "cross" to "crucified one," and a different use of the verb translated "supporting," to "raising up" or "lifting up." Goodacre's emended text would read as follows:

> 39 and as they told the things that they had seen, again they saw three men coming from the tomb, two of them *raising up the one*, and *the crucified one* following them. 40 And the head of the two reached to heaven, but that of him who was led by them overpassed the heavens. 41 And they heard a voice from the heavens, saying, "You preached to the ones who are sleeping?" 42 And a response was heard from the *crucified one*, "Yes."[y]

While this certainly makes more sense and is worthy of consideration, it is a suggestion that cannot be verified.

---

x. Mark Goodacre, "NT Blog: A Walking, Talking Cross or the Walking, Talking Crucified One?," [cited October 18, 2010]. Online: http://ntweblog.blogspot.com/2010/10/walking-talking-cross-or-walking.html.

y. Italics reflect translational changes based on Goodacre's emendations.

TRANSLATION

P.CAIR. 10759 (THE AHKMÎM FRAGMENT)

1.1 But of the Jews none washed his hands,[z] neither Herod nor any one of his judges; and since they did not choose to wash them, Pilate arose. **2** And then Herod the king ordered the Lord to be taken, saying to them that "whatever I ordered you to do to him, you do *it*."

2.3 Now Joseph stood there, the friend of Pilate and of the Lord; and knowing that they were about to crucify him, he came to Pilate and asked for the body[aa] of the Lord for burial. **4** And Pilate sent to Herod and asked for his body. **5** And Herod said, "Brother Pilate, even if no one had asked for his *body*, we should bury him, since the Sabbath also draws near.[ab] For it is written in the law, 'The sun *must* not set on one who has been killed.' "[ac]

3.5 And he delivered[ad] him over to the people before the first day of unleavened bread, their feast. **6** So they took the Lord and pushed him as they ran, and said, "Let us drag the Son of God around, since we have gained power over him." **7** And they clothed him with purple, and set him on a judgment seat, saying, "Judge righteously, O King of Israel."[ae] **8** And one of them brought a crown of thorns and put it on the head of the Lord, **9** and others, standing *there*, were spitting in his eyes, and some struck his cheeks; *still* others stabbed at him with a reed,[af] and some whipped him saying, "With this honor let us honor the Son of God."

4.10 And they brought two criminals, and crucified the Lord between them.[ag] But he kept silent,[ah] as if having no pain. **11** And when they had set the cross straight up, they wrote an inscription *upon it*, "This is the King of Israel."[ai]

---

z. Matt 27:24
aa. Mark 15:43
ab. Luke 23:54
ac. John 19:21; Deut 21:23; Josh 10:27; compare Philo, *de spec. leg.* 28; Jos. *Wars*, 4.5.12.
ad. Mark 15:15
ae. John 19:13
af. Mark 14:65; 15:16–20
ag. Mark 15:24
ah. Mark 14:61; 15:5
ai. Mark 15:24

[12] And they laid his clothes before him, and divided them, and cast lots for them.[aj] [13] But one of the criminals reprimanded them, saying, "We have suffered in this way for the evil that we did, but this man, being the Savior of men, how has he wronged you?"[ak] [14] And being angry with him, they ordered that his legs should not be broken,[al] that he might die in torment *right up* to the end.

5.[15] Now it was noon, and darkness spread over all Judea. And they were troubled and distressed, ₁thinking₁[am] the sun had set while he was still alive; it is written for them that "the sun *must* not set on one who has been killed."[an] [16] And one of them said, "Give him gall with vinegar to drink." And they mixed and gave him to drink.[ao] [17] So they accomplished all things, and heaped up their sins upon their head.[ap] [18] And many went about with lamps, thinking that it was night; and some fell.[aq] [19] And the Lord shouted loudly, saying, "My power, my power, you have left me!"[ar] And having said this he was taken up. [20] And the same hour the veil of the temple of Jerusalem was torn in two.[as]

6.[21] And then they pulled the nails[at] out from the hands of the Lord, and laid him upon the earth. And ₁an earthquake struck,₁[au] and great fear came upon them.[av] [22] Then the sun shone out, and it was found to be the ninth hour.[aw] [23] But the Jews rejoiced, and they gave his body to Joseph to bury it, since he had seen all the good things that he did. [24] So he took the Lord and

---

aj. Mark 15:24
ak. Luke 23:39
al. John 19:31
am. Literally "lest"
an. Mark 15:33; Amos 8:9
ao. Matt 27:34, 48; Psa 68:22
ap. John 19:28, 30
aq. John 11:10
ar. Mark 15:34; Psa 21:2
as. Mark 15:38
at. John 20:25, 27
au. Literally "the whole earth was shaken"
av. Matt 27:51, 54
aw. Mark 15:33

washed him, and wrapped him in linen[ax] and brought him into his own tomb, called Joseph's Garden.[ay]

7.25 Then the Jews and the elders and the priests, knowing what evil they had done to themselves, began to mourn and say, "Woe to our sins! The judgment is at hand, and the end of Jerusalem."[az] 26 And I with my companions was in sorrow; and being wounded at heart we hid ourselves, for we were sought for by them as criminals and as wanting to set the temple on fire. 27 And besides all this, we were fasting, and we sat mourning and weeping night and day until the Sabbath.[ba]

8.28 But the scribes and the Pharisees and elders, being assembled together and hearing that the whole people murmured and mourned, saying, "If these great signs came about at his death, see how righteous he was!"[bb] 29 The elders were afraid and came to Pilate,[bc] petitioning him and saying, 30 "Deliver soldiers to us, that we may guard his tomb for three days, lest his disciples come and steal him away, and the people suppose that he is risen from the dead, and make trouble." 31 So Pilate delivered unto them Petronius the centurion with soldiers to guard the tomb; and elders and scribes came with them to the tomb. 32 And having rolled a great stone against[bd] the centurion and the soldiers, all who were there together placed it at the door of the tomb; 33 and they spread upon it seven seals, and pitched a tent there and kept guard.[be] 34 Now when it was morning, at the dawning of the Sabbath, a crowd came from Jerusalem and the surrounding country to see the tomb, how it had been sealed.

9.35 Now on the night when the Lord's Day was drawing on, as the soldiers kept guard two by two in a watch, there was a great voice in heaven, 36 and

ax. Mark 15:46
ay. John 19:41
az. Luke 23:48
ba. Mark 2:20; 16:10
bb. Luke 23:47
bc. Matt 27:62–66
bd. Some transcriptions have μετὰ, "with." Swete (15) notes the sense here is "to exclude the centurion and the soldiers."
be. Mark 15:46; Matt 27:66

they saw the heavens opened, and two men descend from there with much light and come close unto the tomb. ³⁷ And the stone that had been cast at the door rolled away of itself and made way in part, and the tomb was opened, and both the young men entered in.ᵇᶠ

¹⁰·³⁸ The soldiers, therefore, when they saw it, awakened the centurion and the elders (for they were also there keeping watch); ³⁹ and as they told the things that they had seen, again they saw three men coming from the tomb, two of them supporting the other, and a cross following them. ⁴⁰ And the head of the two reached to heaven, but that of him who was led by them overpassed the heavens. ⁴¹ And they heard a voice from the heavens, saying, "You preached to the ones who are sleeping?"ᵇᵍ ⁴² And a response was heard from the cross, "Yes."

¹¹·⁴³ Therefore they took counsel with one another to go and reveal these things to Pilate. ⁴⁴ And while they considered this, the heavens again appeared to open, and a man descended and entered into the tomb. ⁴⁵ When they saw this, those of the centurion's company hastened by night to Pilate, leaving the tomb that they were guarding, and told all that they had seen, greatly distressed and saying, "Truly he was the Son of God."ᵇʰ ⁴⁶ Pilate answered and said, "I am clean from the blood of the Son of God, but this was your pleasure."ᵇⁱ ⁴⁷ Then they all came near and petitioned him, and asked him to order the centurion and the soldiers to say nothing as to the things that they had seen. ⁴⁸ "For it is expedient for us," they said, "to be guilty of a very great sin before God, and not to fall into the hands of the people of the Jews and be stoned."ᵇʲ ⁴⁹ Pilate therefore commanded the centurion and the soldiers to say nothing.ᵇᵏ

---

bf. Matt 28:1
bg. Swete notes this "is probably not a question addressed to the Cross, but the revelation of a fact" (19).
bh. Mark 15:39
bi. Matt 27:24
bj. John 11:50
bk. Matt 28:11–15

12.50 Now at dawn on the Lord's Day Mary Magdalene,bl a disciple of the Lord—afraid because of the Jews,bm since they were inflamed with wrath, she had not done at the tomb of the Lord what women ₁typically do₁bn for those who die and who are dear to them—51 took with her female friends, and came to the tomb where he was laid. 52 And they feared lest the Jews should see them, and they said, "Although we could not weep and mourn him on the day when he was crucified, let us do so now at his tomb. 53 But who will roll away the stone for us that was laid at the door of the tomb, that we may enter in and sit by him, and do the things that are due? 54 For the stone was great,bo and we fear lest anyone see us. And if we cannot, even though we should leave at the door the things that we bring for his memorial, we will weep and mourn him until we come to our house."

13.55 So they went and found the tomb open, and they came near and stooped down to look in there. And they saw a young man sitting in the midst of the tomb, fair and clothed with a robe exceedingly bright, who said to them, 56 "Why have you come? Whom do you seek? He who was crucified? He is risen and gone. But if you do not believe, stoop down and look in, and see the place where he lay, that he is not here; for he has risen and gone away from there, where he was sent." 57 Then the women fled, being afraid.bp

14.58 Now it was the last day of unleavened bread, and many went out of the city returning to their houses, the feast being at an end. 59 And we the twelve disciples of the Lord wept and were in sorrow, and every man returned to his house grieving for what had come to pass. 60 But I, Simon Peter, and Andrew my brother, taking our nets we went to the sea;bq and there was with us Levi the son of Alphaeus whom the Lord ...

---

bl. Matt 28:1
bm. John 20:19
bn. Literally "are wont to do"
bo. Mark 16:3
bp. Mark 16:1–8
bq. John 21:1

P.OXY. 2949

Reading Translation

FRAGMENT 1: Recto. ... But he stood there, Joseph, the friend of Pilate, and....
And knowing that he had ordered him to be crucified, coming to Pilate he
asked ... the body for burial. Pilate sent to Herod to ask him for the body
to be given, saying: ... I asked ... him ... that ...

Verso. [blank]

FRAGMENT 2: Recto. ... of me ... Pilate ... someone him ...

Verso. [blank]

Line Translation

FRAGMENT 1: Recto

1 [...]
2 [...]
3 [...]
4 [... But he stood there,]
5 [Joseph,] the friend of P[i]la[t]e, a[nd ...]
6 [And know]ing that he had ordered him [to be cru-]
7 [cified, comi]ng to Pilat[e he asked]
8 [...] the body for burial. [Pilate]
9 [sent to Her]od to as[k him for]
10 [the body to be gi]ven, sayi[ng:]
11 [...] I asked [...]
12 [...] him [...]
13 [...] that [...]

Verso. [blank]

FRAGMENT 2: Recto

1 [...] of me [...]

2 Pil[ate ...]
3 someone h[im ...]
4 [...]
5 [...]

Verso. [blank]

P.Oxy. 4009

Reading Translation

Fragment 1: Recto

... and ... harvest. But you be innocent as the doves and wise like the snakes. You will be like sheep in the midst of wolves." I said to him, "What if, then, we are torn apart?" And answering, he said to me, "The wolves, having torn apart the sheep, no longer can possibly do anything. So I myself say to you, have no fear of those who kill you, and after killing are no longer able to do anything.... having ...

Verso. [blank]

Line Translation

Fragment 1: Recto

1   [...]
2   [...]
3   [...] an[d.].
4   [...] harvest
5   [But you be inno]cent as the [do-]
6   [ves a]nd wis[e]
7   [like the snakes.] You will be like
8   [sheep in the mi]dst of wolves."
9   [I said to h]im, "What if, the(n),
10 [we are torn] apart?"
11 [And answering,] he said to me, "The
12 [wolves, having torn] apart the

13 [sheep, no] longer to him no-
14 [thing can possibly] be done. S-
15 [o myself I say to] you, [no] have
16 [fear of tho]se who k[il-]
17 [l yo]u, and [after]
18 [killing] no lon[ger to]
19 [do are ab]le [nothin(g).]
20 [. h]aving[...]
21 [...]...[...]

Verso. [blank]

SELECT BIBLIOGRAPHY

Bernhard, Andrew. *Other Early Christian Gospels: A Critical Edition of the Surviving Greek Manuscripts.* London: T&T Clark International, 2007.

Ehrman, Bart D., and Zlatko Pleše. *The Apocryphal Gospels: Texts and Translations.* Oxford: Oxford University Press, 2010.

Goodacre, Mark. "A Walking, Talking Cross or the Walking, Talking Crucified One?" NT Blog, October 18, 2010. Online: http://ntweblog.blogspot.com/2010/10/walking-talking-cross-or-walking.html.

Grenfell, Bernard P., and Arthur S. Hunt, eds. *Catalogue Général des Antiquitiés Égyptiennes du Musée du Caire, Nos. 10001–10869: Greek Papyri.* Oxford: Oxford University Press, 1903.

Harnack, A. *Bruchstücke des Evangeliums und der Apokalypse des Petrus.* Leipzig: J. C. Hinrichs'sche Buchhandlung, 1893.

Lührmann, D., and E. Schlarb. *Fragmente apokryph gewordener Evangelien in Griechischer und lateinischer Sprache. Marburger theologische Studien* 59. Marburg: N. G. Elwert, 2000.

Mirecki, Paul Allan. "Peter, Gospel of." *ABD* 5:279–81.

Robinson, J. A. "The Gospel According to Peter." *The Gospel According to Peter and the Revelation of Peter: Two Lectures on the Newly Recovered Fragments Together with the Greek Texts.* Edited by M. R. James and J. A. Robinson. London: C. J. Clay, 1892.

Swete, H. B. *The Akhmîm Fragment of the Apocryphal Gospel of Peter.* London: Macmillan, 1893.

The Gospel of Thomas
(Greek Portions)

INTRODUCTION

Writings from the first few centuries of the Church occasionally mention a gospel attributed to Thomas,[a] the disciple of Jesus. While the *Infancy Gospel of Thomas*[b] is known from various manuscripts and editions, a gospel written in the name of Thomas recording events and sayings from Jesus' ministry was not extant. This changed with the discovery of the Nag Hammadi cache of codices in 1945, in which a Coptic edition of the *Gospel of Thomas* was found.

With the Coptic edition of the *Gospel of Thomas*, it was soon discovered that within the Oxyrhynchus papyri, Grenfell and Hunt had already transcribed and published Greek editions of sayings from the *Gospel of Thomas* in P.Oxy. 1, 654 and 655. They had isolated these papyri as examples of non-canonical gospel manuscripts and published them individually. P.Oxy. 1 was published as ΛΟΓΙΑ ΙΗΣΟΥ: *Sayings of Our Lord from an Early Greek Papyri* in 1897;[c] and P.Oxy. 1, 654, and 655 were published as *New Sayings of Jesus and Fragments of a Lost Gospel from Oxyrhynchus* in 1904.[d]

---

a. Bart D. Ehrman and Zlatko Pleše, *The Apocryphal Gospels: Texts and Translations* (Oxford: Oxford University Press, 2010), 303–04.

b. See the introduction to the *Infancy Gospel of Thomas*.

c. Bernard P. Grenfell and Arthur S. Hunt, ΛΟΓΙΑ ΙΗΣΟΥ: *Sayings of Our Lord from an Early Greek Papyri* (London: Henry Frowde, 1897).

d. Bernard P. Grenfell and Arthur S. Hunt, *New Sayings of Jesus and Fragment of a Lost Gospel from Oxyrhynchus* (London: Oxford University Press, 1904).

CONTENT

The *Gospel of Thomas* (*Gos. Thom.*) is the most complete example of a "sayings gospel"—a collection of sayings or *logia* of Jesus, sometimes including interaction with his disciples. These three sets of fragments from Oxyrhynchus contain the following sayings from *Gos. Thom.*:

- P.Oxy. 654: Gospel prologue and sayings 1–7.

- P.Oxy. 1: Sayings 26–30, 77b, 31–33.

- P.Oxy. 655: Sayings 36–39.

The sayings themselves have several points of contact with the canonical Gospel text.

P.Oxy. 654

P.Oxy. 654 is dated to the "middle or late third century."[e] The *Gos. Thom.* material is written on the verso of a papyrus roll,[f] including symbols that denote (where extant) the sayings' boundaries. The recto contains what appears to be a land survey.[g] What is important, P.Oxy. 654 contains the prologue to *Gos. Thom.*, which frames the gospel: "These are the hidden words, those spoken by the living Jesus and written down by Judas who is also Thomas."

In their translation of the reconstructed prologue,[h] Grenfell and Hunt suggested "wonderful words" where, with the hindsight provided by the Coptic edition, it is now known that "hidden words" is proper. To their credit, Grenfell and Hunt knew an adjective needed to be there; their intuition was likely colored by what sort of gospel they thought they were working with.[i]

Sayings 1–5 are a series of sayings of Jesus with no other interaction. Saying 1 does not explicitly identify Jesus as the speaker, but the ambiguity

---

e. Andrew Bernhard, *Other Early Christian Gospels: A Critical Edition of the Surviving Greek Manuscripts* (London: T&T Clark, 2007), 18.

f. Grenfell and Hunt, *New Sayings of Jesus*, 9.

g. Ibid.

h. Ibid., 12.

i. Also to their credit, the educated guesses of Grenfell and Hunt in their translations seem to be correct or at least within the proper realm more often than they are wrong. In other words, given what they had, it is amazing how much they got right.

is easily resolved by the prologue. Sayings 2–5 specify Jesus as the speaker. Each of these sayings is a wisdom saying. While comprehensible, they also have some aspect of mystery.

Saying 6 is initiated by the disciples, who ask Jesus about fasting, praying, acting mercifully (some translations render this as giving alms), and laws having to do with food. Jesus' response is generic and somewhat mysterious, telling the disciples not to lie and not to do things they hate because all things will be revealed.

P.Oxy. 1

P.Oxy. 1 is dated to the "late second or early third century."[j] It is a single page from a codex, with well-preserved writing on both sides. It is probably the eleventh page of a codex, indicating a volume of some size.[k]

Each saying in P.Oxy. 1 begins with "Jesus said," and all are wisdom sayings. Some have ties to canonical material (e.g., Saying 26 and Matt 7:3), others are mixed (e.g., Saying 31a and John 4:44), and still others sound like they should have some canonical witness, but do not (e.g., Saying 27).

P.Oxy. 655

P.Oxy. 655 is dated to the "third century."[l] It is a collection of eight fragments labeled with letters a—h. Fragments a, b and c are from the same papyrus leaf and contain witness to the Greek of sayings 36–39, although the extant material of saying 38 cannot be reconstructed beyond "Jesus said."

Most consider fragment d to witness Saying 24,[m] but the extant material consists of less than 20 letters dispersed across five lines, with many of the letters uncertain. It seems best to note the possibility, but not include the material for transcription and translation. Fragments e, f and g are too small and uncertain to transcribe.

Saying 36 has strong similarities to Matt 6:25, 31 and Luke 12:22. Saying 37, which is incomplete in P.Oxy. 655, is initiated by the disciples and has no direct parallel in synoptic material. Saying 39 appears to be a mixture of Luke 11:52 and Matt 10:16.

---

j. Bernhard, *Other Early Christian Gospels*, 12.

k. Grenfell and Hunt, *New Sayings of Jesus*, 21; Bernhard, *Other Early Christian Gospels*, 18.

l. Bernhard, *Other Early Christian Gospels*, 18.

m. Ibid., 32–33; Ehrman and Pleše, *The Apocryphal Gospels*, 340–41.

TRANSLATION

Translations of P.Oxy. 1, 654, 655 are from transcriptions initially based upon the editions of Grenfell and Hunt,[n] thoroughly updated and revised based on Attridge[o] (the edition used by Ehrman and Pleše[p]) and Bernhard.[q] Reconstructions in the transcriptions are based on Attridge and Bernhard in consultation with the available Coptic sources.

P.Oxy. 654

Reading Translation

Fragment 1: Verso. **Prologue:** These are the hidden words, those spoken by the living Jesus and written down by Judas who is also Thomas.

Saying 1: And he said, "Whoever finds the interpretation of these sayings will not taste death.

Saying 2: Jesus said, "Let the one who seeks not stop to seek until he finds. And when he finds he will be amazed, and when he has been amazed he will rule, and when he has ruled, he will rest."

Saying 3: Jesus said, "If those who lead you say to you, 'Behold, the kingdom is in the sky,' the birds of the sky will come ahead of you. But if they say that it is under the earth, ... the fish of the sea ... you. And the kingdom of God is inside of you and outside, whoever knows himself will find this. And when you know yourselves you will see that you are the children of the living father. But if you do not know yourselves, you are in poverty and you are poverty."

---

n. Grenfell and Hunt, ΛΟΓΙΑ ΙΗΣΟΥ: *Sayings of Our Lord*; Grenfell and Hunt, *New Sayings of Jesus*.

o. H. W. Attridge, "The Greek Fragments," in *Nag Hammadi Codex II, 2–7 together with XII.2**, Brit Lib. Or 4926 (1) and P.Oxy. 1, 654, 655, ed. B. Layton (Leiden: Brill, 1989), 95–128.

p. Ehrman and Pleše, *The Apocryphal Gospels*, 303–349.

q. Bernhard, *Other Early Christian Gospels*, 16–48.

Saying 4: Jesus said, "A man old in days Will not hesitate to ask a child of seven days about the place of life, and he will live. For many who are first will be last and the last first. And they will become one."

Saying 5: Jesus said, "Know what is before your eyes and what is hidden from you will be revealed to you, for nothing is hidden which will not be made visible, and nothing is buried that will not be raised."

Saying 6: His disciples were questioning him and saying, "How shall we fast? And how shall we pray? And how shall we act mercifully? And what rules shall we follow regarding food?" Jesus said, "Do not lie and that which you hate do not do ... of the truth ... For nothing is hidden which will not appear.

Saying 7: Blessed is ... lion will be ...

Line Translation

FRAGMENT 1: Verso

1   These are the words, the [hidden ones, those spok-]
2   en by Jesus the living a[nd written down by Judas who is]
3   also Thomas. And he said [whoever the interpret-]
4   ation sayings of the[se finds death]
5   not will taste. § [Jesus said]
6   "not Let stop the one who se[eks to seek until]
7   he finds. And when he finds [he will be amazed and when he]
8   has been amazed he will rule, an[d when he has ruled, he will]
9   rest." § Said J[esus, "If]
10   those who lead you [say to you, 'Behold,]
11   the kingdom is in the sk[y,' of you will come ahead]
12   the birds of the sk[y. But if they say t-]
13   hat under the earth it i[s ...]
14   the fish of the se[a ...]
15   ... you. And the king[dom of God]
16   inside of you [i]s [and outside, whoever himself]
17   knows this will fi[nd. And when you]

18 yourselves know [you will see that the children]
19 you are of the father of the liv[ing. But if not]
20 you know yourselves, in [poverty you are]
21 and you are pov[erty." § Jesus says]
22 "Will not hesitate a ma[n old in da-]
23 ys to ask a ch[ild of seven da-]
24 ys about the place o[f life and he will]
25 live. For many who are f[irst will be last and]
26 the last first. And [into one they will be]
27 come." Jesus said, § "K[now what is bef-]
28 ore your eyes and [what is hidden]
29 from you will be reveal[ed to you, for nothing i-]
30 s hidden which not visi[ble will be made,]
31 and buried that n[ot will be raised."]
32 Questioning him th[e disciples of him and]
33 [sa]ying, "How shall we fa[st? And how shall we]
34 [pr]ay? And how [mercifully shall we]
35 [act? A]nd what rules shall we foll[ow regarding fo-]
36 [o]d?" § Jesus said, ["Do not lie and th]
37 [at which you] hate not do d[o ...]
38 [... of t]he tr[u]th. [... nothing]
39 [for i]s h[i]dd[en which not appear]
40 [will. Bl]ess[ed] is [...]
41 [... li]on will b[e ...]
42 [...]. [...]

P.Oxy. 1

Reading Translation

FRAGMENT 1: Verso. **Saying 26:** "and then you will see clearly to take out the speck, the one in your brother's eye."

Saying 27: Jesus said, "Unless you fast to the world, you will not find the kingdom of God, and if you do not keep the sabbath as the sabbath, you will not see the Father."

Saying 28: Jesus said, "I stood in the midst of the world and in the flesh I appeared to them. And I found everyone was drunk, and I found nobody was thirsty among them. And my soul is afflicted for the children of humanity because they are blind in their hearts and do not see ..."

Recto. **Saying 29:** "... of the poverty."

Saying 30 and 77b: Jesus said, "Wherever there are three, they are godless. And where one is alone, I say I myself am with him. Lift up the stone, and there you will find me. Split the wood and I myself am there."

Saying 31: Jesus said, "A prophet is not welcome in his homeland, neither does a doctor do healings among those who know him."

Saying 32: Jesus said, "A city built on top of a high mountain and well provisioned is neither able to fall or to be hidden."

Saying 33: Jesus said, "You hear in the one ear you the ..."

Line Translation

FRAGMENT 1: Verso

1   "and then you will see clearly
2   to take out the speck,
3   the one in the eye
4   of your brother." Said
5   Jesus, "Unless you fas-
6   t to the world, not
7   will you find the kingd-
8   om of God, and if not
9   you do keep the sabbath as the sab-
10   bath, not you will see the
11   Father." Jesus said, "I stood
12   in the midst of the world
13   and in the flesh I appeared
14   to them. And I found al-

15 l being drunk, and
16 nobody I found were thirs-
17 ty among them and is
18 afflicted my soul for
19 the children of humanity
20 because blind they are in the hear-
21 t thei[r] and not do
22 [see ...]

Recto

1   [....]. [.of] the poverty."
2   [Sa]id [Jesus, "Wh]erever there are
3   [thr]e[e] the[y ar]e godless. And
4   [w]here one is alone,
5   [I s]ay I myself am with h-
6   i[m]. Li[f]t up the stone,
7   and there you will find me.
8   Split the wood and I
9   there I am." Jesus said, "No-
10 t is welcome a pro-
11 phet in the homeland of
12 h[i]m, neither does a doctor do
13 healings among those
14 who know him."
15 Jesus said, "A city bui-
16 lt on top of
17 [a mou]ntain high and well
18 provisioned neither to
19 [f]all is able nor to
20 [be] hidden." Jesus said, "You hear
21 [i]n the one ear you the

P.OXY. 655ᴿ

Reading Translation

FRAGMENT A-C: Recto Column 1. **Saying 36:** Jesus said, "Do not be anxious from early morning until late in the day, or from evening until early morning, or for your food, what you will eat, or for your robe, what you will wear. You are much better than the lillies that do not card or spin. Having no clothing, what do you wear, even you? Who could add to your life? He himself will give you your clothing."

Saying 37: His disciples said to him, "When will you be revealed? And when will we see you?" He said, "When you remove your clothes and are not ashamed...."

Recto Column 2. **Saying 38:** ... Jesus said ... and ... and ...,

Saying 39: Jesus said, "The Pharisees and the scribes have taken the keys of knowledge and hidden them. Neither have they entered nor have they permitted those entering to enter. But you, become wise like snakes and innocent like doves...."

Line Translation

FRAGMENT A-C: Recto Column 1

    0   [Jesus said, "Do not be anxio-]
    1   [us fr]om early morning unt[il late,]
    2   [o]r from even[ing]
    3   [until ear]ly morning, or [the]
    4   [food of] you, what you
    5   [will eat, or] the r[o-]
    6   [be your] what you
    7   [will] wear. [Mu]ch be[t-]
    8   [ter] than [you are] the [lil-]

---

r. Fragments d, e, f, g, and h have not been transcribed.

9   lies tha[t no]t do ca[r-]

10   d or s[pi]n. N[ot]

11   hing havi[ng c]lo[t-]

12   hing, what do yo[u wear], even

13   you? Who could add

14   to the life

15   of you? Himse[lf he w]ill give

16   to you the clothing to y-

17   ou." They said to

18   him the disciples of him

19   "When you reveal-

20   ed will be? And when

21   you will we see?" He said,

22   "When you remove your clothes and

23   not are ashamed...."

Recto Column 2

1   [...]

2   sa[id Jesus ...]

3   [...]

4   [...]

5   [...]

6   an[d ...]

7   [...]

8   an[d ...]

9   [...]

10   [...]

11   [... Said]

12   [Jesus, "The Pharisees]

13   [and the scribes]

14   hav[e taken the keys]

15   of [knowledge and h-]

16   idd[en them. Neither]

17   have they enter[ed nor those]

18   entering [into have they]

19   permitted [to enter. You]

20 but be[come wis-]
21 e li[ke the snakes and in-]
22 noce[nt like do-]
23 ve[s]...."

SELECT BIBLIOGRAPHY

Attridge, H. W. "The Greek Fragments." Pages 95–128 in *Nag Hammadi Codex II, 2–7 together with XII.2*, Brit Lib. Or 4926 (1) and P.Oxy. 1, 654, 655.* Edited by B. Layton. Leiden: Brill, 1989.

Bernhard, Andrew. *Other Early Christian Gospels: A Critical Edition of the Surviving Greek Manuscripts.* London: T&T Clark, 2007.

Ehrman, Bart D., and Zlatko Pleše. *The Apocryphal Gospels: Texts and Translations.* Oxford: Oxford University Press, 2010.

Grenfell, Bernard P., and Arthur S. Hunt. *New Sayings of Jesus and Fragment of a Lost Gospel from Oxyrhynchus.* London: Oxford University Press, 1904.

———. ΛΟΓΙΑ ΙΗΣΟΥ: *Sayings of Our Lord from an Early Greek Papyrus.* London: Henry Frowde, 1897.

– The Gospel of Nicodemus (*Acts of Pilate*) and Descent of Christ into Hades

INTRODUCTION

The *Gospel of Nicodemus* (*Gos. Nic.*) has been transmitted in two parts, with the first (chapters 1–16) known as the *Acts of Pilate* and the second (chapters 17–27) known as the *Descent of Christ into Hades*. Thus, in their introduction to *Gos. Nic.*, Ehrman and Pleše write, "One of the complications of this writing is knowing even what to call it."[a] Further complicating matters is that the manuscript and versional evidence provide two different editions of the writing, thanks to Tischendorf now known as *Acts of Pilate A*[b] and *Acts of Pilate B*.[c] *Acts of Pilate A* does not, in its Greek witnesses, contain the *Descent of Christ into Hades* (chapters 17–27), but *Acts of Pilate B* does.

All available manuscript evidence is late. There are no Greek witnesses of *Acts of Pilate A* before the 12th century, although Latin witnesses date to the 5th century (for chapters 1–16) and the 9th century (for chapters 17–27).[d] Klauck notes:

> By ca. 378, Epiphanius of Salamis clearly knows Christian Acts of Pilate, which existed in a variety of divergent versions (*Panarion* 50.1.5–8). This allows us to date the composition of the Acts of Pilate to the first decades of the fourth century; the author will have drawn on older material. For chs. 17–27 (the descent into hell), we must be

---

a. Bart D. Ehrman and Zlatko Pleše, *The Apocryphal Gospels: Texts and Translations* (Oxford: Oxford University Press, 2010), 419.
b. C. von Tischendorf, *Evangelia Apocrypha*, 2nd ed. (Leipzig: Mendelssohn, 1876), 210–286.
c. Ibid. 287–322.
d. Hans-Josef Klauck, *Apocryphal Gospels: An Introduction* (London: T&T Clark, 2004), 90.

content with a more general dating to the fifth or sixth century, and the prior history of the material must remain an open question.[e]

By all accounts, *Gos. Nic.* was written well after the events it describes, although it purports to come from Nicodemus (John 3:1–21; 7:50–52; 19:38–42). The *Gospel of Nicodemus* is based on the events surrounding Jesus' death and resurrection in the canonical Gospels but expands on them, providing unknown and unknowable details. It fills in many holes left in the canonical narrative with details that reinforce the deity of Jesus.

CONTENT

The text describes itself as a translation of a document originally written in Hebrew, although in reality it was composed in Greek.[f] Readers of the canonical Gospels will be familiar with the basic story and content, to which there are several expansions. Taking *Acts of Pilate* A (chapters 1–16) and the *Descent of Christ into Hades* (chapters 17–27) as a whole, there are three parts to the story:

- Jesus' Trial and Death (1–11)

- Joseph of Arimathea and Nicodemus (12–16)

- The Descent of Christ into Hades (17–27)

The first two parts of the story comprise the *Acts of Pilate*, and roughly follow the progression of the story as portrayed in the Gospels. The story draws from the Scriptures frequently, with both allusions and outright citations. Most are from the Gospels, but knowledge of major prophecies from the Hebrew Bible is evident in the *Descent of Christ into Hades*. Below is a list that focuses on quotations, direct allusions, and where the words of the Scriptures are put into the mouths of participants in *Gos. Nic.*

Acts of Pilate A

- 1.3 == Matt 21:1–10; Mark 1:1–11; Luke 19:28–39; John 12:12–19

---

e. Ibid. 91.

f. Ehrman and Pleše, *The Apocryphal Gospels*, 420.

- 2.1 == Matt 27:19

- 3.1 == John 18:30, 31

- 3.2 == John 18:33–38

- 4.1 == John 18:38; Matt 26:61; Mark 14:58; Matt 27:24–26

- 4.3 == John 18:31

- 4.4 == John 19:7

- 5.1 == Acts 5:38–39

- 6.1 == Matt 9:1–8; Mark 2:1–12; Luke 5:17–26; John 5:1–13

- 6.2 == Matt 20:29–34; Mark 10:46–52; Luke 18:35–43

- 7.1 == Matt 9:20–22; Mark 5:25–34; Luke 8:43–48

- 9.1 == Matt 27:15–23; Mark 15:6–15; Luke 23:18–25; John 18:39–40; 19:23

- 9.3 == Matt 2:7–18

- 9.4 == Matt 27:24–26

- 10.1 == Luke 23:34; Matt 27:38–43; Mark 15:27–32; Luke 23:35–38

- 10.2 == Luke 23:39–43

- 11.1 == Luke 23:44–48

- 11.3 == Matt 27:57–61; Mark 15:42–46; Luke 23:50–53; John 19:38–42

- 12.1 == Rom 12:19 citing Deut 32:35; Matt 27:24–26

- 13.1 == Matt 28:2–4; 5–7

- 13.3 == Matt 28:12–14

- 14.1 == Mark 16:15–18

- 15.1 == 2 Kgs 2:1–18

- 16.2 == Luke 2:28–35

- 16.6 == Deut 19:15; Gen 5:24; Deut 34:5–6; Luke 2:34; Exod 23:20–21

- 16.7 == Luke 2:34; Deut 21:23; Jer 10:11

Descent of Christ into Hades

- 18.1 == Isa 9:1–2

- 18.2 == John 1:29; Matt 3:16–17

- 20.1 == Matt 26:38

- 21.1 == Psa 23:7 (LXX)

- 21.2 == Psa 23:7 (LXX); Isa 26:19; 1 Cor 15:55, referring to Isa 25:8

- 21.3 == Psa 23:8 (LXX)

- 24.2 == Psa 118:26 (LXX)

- 26.1 == Luke 23:43

DESCENT OF CHRIST INTO HADES

The *Descent of Christ into Hades* relies on a few hints given in the NT to create an account of Christ cleaning out Hades and binding Satan. Simeon and his two sons, raised from the dead at Christ's death (compare Matt 27:52–53), tell a story of the saints in Hades, from Adam to John the Baptist, and their release from Hades and return to Paradise. In the process, Christ commands Hades (personified in the narrative) to bind Satan and keep him secured.

TRANSLATION

The translation is a reworking of M. R. James' translation of *Gos. Nic.*[g] and *The Descent of Christ into Hell*,[h] edited in consultation with Tischendorf's *Acta Pilati A*[i] and *Descensus Christi ad Inferos*[j]

---

g. M. R. James, *The Apocryphal New Testament* (Oxford: Clarendon, 1924), 95–115.
h. Ibid., 119–146.
i. Tischendorf, *Evangelia Apocrypha*, 210–286.
j. Ibid., 323–332.

Public Records of Our Lord Jesus Christ
Done in the Time of Pontius Pilate

PROLOGUE

I, Ananias, the Protector, of praetorian rank, schooled in the law, from the divine scriptures recognized our Lord Jesus Christ and came near to him by faith, and was counted worthy of holy baptism. And I sought out the public records[k] that were made at that season in the time of our master Jesus Christ, which the Jews deposited with Pontius Pilate, and found the public records *written* in Hebrew, and by the good pleasure of God I translated them into Greek for the informing of all those who call upon the name of our Lord Jesus Christ. *This was done* in the reign of our Lord Flavius Theodosius, in the seventeenth year, and of Flavius Valentinianus the sixth, in the ninth indiction.

All you therefore who read this and translate[l] it into other books, remember me and pray for me that God will be gracious to me and be merciful to my sins that I have sinned against him.

Peace be to those who read and who hear these things and to their servants. Amen.

In the fifteenth[m] year of the rule of Tiberius Caesar, emperor of the Romans, and of Herod, king of Galilee, in the nineteenth year of his rule, on the eighth of the Kalends of April, which is the 25th of March, in the consulate of Rufus and Rubellio, in the fourth year of the two hundred and second Olympiad, when Joseph (who is Caiaphas) was high priest of the Jews:

These are the things that, after the cross and passion of the Lord, Nicodemus recorded and delivered to the high priest and the rest of the Jews. And the same Nicodemus ⌊wrote them down⌋[n] in Hebrew.

---

k. See LSJ, ὑπόμνημα II 4, "*minutes* of the proceedings of a public body, *public records*"
l. Or "copy"
m. Some versions have "nineteenth"
n. Literally "set them forth"

1.1 For the chief priests and scribes assembled in council: Annas and Caiaphas and Semes and Dathaes and Gamaliel, Judas, Levi and Nepthalim, Alexander and Jairus and the rest of the Jews came to Pilate accusing Jesus of many deeds, saying, "We know this man, that he is the son of Joseph the carpenter, born of Mary, and he calls himself the Son of God and a king; on top of that he even profanes the Sabbaths, and he would destroy the law of our ancestors."

Pilate said, "And what are the things he does, and *what* does he want to destroy?"

The Jews said, "We have a law that we should not heal any man on the Sabbath. But this one, by evil deeds, has healed the lame and the crippled, the withered and the blind and the paralytic, the speechless and those who were possessed, on the Sabbath day!"

Pilate said to them, "By what evil deeds?"

They said to him, "He is a swindler, and by Beelzebub° the prince of the demons he casts out demons, and they are all subject to him."

Pilate said to them, "This is not *possible*, to cast out demons by an unclean spirit, only by the god Asclepius *can this be done*."

2 The Jews said to Pilate, "We urge your greatness that he appear before your judgment seat and be heard." And calling to them, Pilate said, "Tell me, how can I, a governor, question a king?" They said to him, "We do not say that he is a king, but he said it of himself."

And Pilate, calling the messenger, said to him, "Let Jesus be brought here gently." And the messenger went out, and upon recognizing him, he worshiped *him* and took his handkerchief and spread it upon the ground and said to him, "Lord, walk here and enter in, for the governor summons you." And the Jews, upon seeing what the messenger had done, cried out against

---

o. Gk. *Beelzeboul*

Pilate, saying, "Why did you not summon him to come in by a herald, but by a messenger? For the messenger, upon seeing him, worshiped *him* and spread out his kerchief on the ground and had him walk *in* like a king!"

³ And Pilate, calling for the messenger, said to him, "Why have you done this, spreading out your kerchief on the ground, and made Jesus to walk upon it?" The messenger said to him, "Lord governor, when you sent me to Jerusalem to Alexander, I saw *him* sitting upon a donkey, and the children of the Hebrews held branches in their hands and cried out, and others spread their garments beneath him, saying, "Save *us* now, one in the highest *heavens*. Blessed is he who comes in the name of the Lord."[p]

⁴ The Jews cried out, saying to the messenger, "The children of the Hebrews cried out in Hebrew. How then ⌊do you know what they said⌋[q] in Greek?" The messenger said to them, "I asked one of the Jews and said, 'What is it that they cry out in Hebrew?' And he interpreted it to me."

Pilate said to them, "And what[r] did they cry out in Hebrew?" The Jews said to him, "*hōsanna membromē barouchamma adonai*."[s] Pilate said to them, "And the Hosanna and the rest, how is it interpreted?" The Jews said to him, "Save *us* now, one in the highest *heavens*. Blessed is he who comes in the name of the Lord." Pilate said to them, "If you yourselves bear witness of the words that were said of the children, how has the messenger sinned?" And they held their peace.

The governor said to the messenger, "Go out and bring him in however you please." And the messenger went out and did ⌊as he did before⌋[t] and said to Jesus, "Lord, enter in. The governor calls you."

⁵ Now when Jesus entered in, and the standard-bearers were holding the standards, the images of the standards bowed and worshiped Jesus. And

p. Matt 21:1–10; Mark 11:1–11; Luke 19:28–39; John 12:12–19
q. Literally "have you it"
r. Or "how"
s. The Greek is a transliteration of the Hebrew
t. Literally "after the former manner"

when the Jews saw the manner of the standards, how they bowed themselves and worshiped Jesus, they cried out even louder against the standard-bearers. But Pilate said to the Jews, "Are you not amazed that the images bowed themselves and worshiped Jesus?" The Jews said to Pilate, "We saw how the standard-bearers made them bow and worship him." And the governor called for the standard-bearers and said to them, "Why did you do this?" They said to Pilate, "We are Greeks and temple servants, and how could we worship him? For indeed, while we held the images they bowed by themselves and worshiped him."

⁶ Pilate said to the rulers of the synagogue and the elders of the people, "You choose strong and powerful men and let them hold the standards, and let us see if they bow by themselves." And the elders of the Jews took twelve strong and powerful men and made them hold the standards by sixes, and they were set before the judgment seat of the governor. And Pilate said to the messenger, "Take him out of the judgment hall and bring him in again however you desire." And Jesus went out of the judgment hall, he and the messenger. And Pilate called those who previously held the images and said to them, "I have sworn by the safety of Caesar that if the standards do not bow when Jesus enters in, I will cut off your heads."

And the governor commanded Jesus to enter in the second time. And the messenger did ₍as he did before₎ᵘ and greatly urged Jesus, that he would walk upon his kerchief. And he walked upon it and entered in. And when he had entered, the standards bowed themselves again and worshiped Jesus.

²·¹ Upon seeing it, Pilate became afraid, and tried to get up from the judgment seat. And while he was still thinking about getting up, his wife sent to him, saying, "You have nothing to do with this righteous one, for I have suffered many things because of him through the night."ᵛ And Pilate called to himself all the Jews, and said to them, "You know that my wife fears God and prefers the customs of the Jews, with you?" They said to him, "Yes, we know." Pilate said to them, "See, my wife has sent to me, saying,

---

u. Literally "after the former manner"
v. Matt 27:19

"You have nothing to do with this righteous one, for I have suffered many things because of him through the night." But answering, the Jews said to Pilate, "Did we not tell you that he is a sorcerer? Look, he has sent a dream to your wife."

² And Pilate called Jesus to him and said to him, "Why do these people testify against you? Do you have nothing to say?" But Jesus said, "If they had no power they would say nothing; for each one has power over his own mouth, to speak good or evil. They shall see to it."

³ And answering, the elders of the Jews said to Jesus, "What shall we see? First, that you were born of fornication; second, that your birth in Bethlehem was *the cause of* the slaying of children; third, that your father Joseph and your mother Mary fled into Egypt because they had no confidence before the people."

⁴ Some of those who stood by, devout ones of the Jews, said, "We do not say that he came of fornication; but we know that Joseph was betrothed to Mary, and he was not born of fornication." Pilate said to those Jews who said that he came of fornication, "This your saying is not true because there was a betrothal, just as even these your own countrymen say." Annas and Caiaphas said to Pilate, "Our whole multitude cries out—and we are not believed—that he was born of fornication, yet these are proselytes and disciples of his." And Pilate called Annas and Caiaphas to himself and said to them, "What are proselytes?" They said to him, "They were born children of Greeks, and now they have become Jews." Those who said that he was not born of fornication—Lazarus, Asterius, Antonius, Jacob, Amnes, Zeras, Samuel, Isaac, Phineas, Crispus, Agrippus,ʷ and Judas—said, "We were not born proselytes, but we are children of Jews and we speak the truth, for we were also present at the betrothal of Joseph and Mary."

⁵ And Pilate summoned those twelve men who said that he was not born of fornication, and said to them, "I implore you by the salvation of Caesar: is it true what you say, that he was not born of fornication?" They said to

---

w. Or "Agrippa"

Pilate, "We have a law that we make no oath, because it is sin. But let them make an oath by the salvation of Caesar that it is not as we have said, and we will be guilty of death." Pilate said to Annas and Caiaphas, "Can you answer nothing to these things?" Annas and Caiaphas said to Pilate, "These twelve men are believed, that he was not born of fornication. Our whole multitude cries out that he was born of fornication, and is a sorcerer, and says that he is the Son of God and a king, and we are not believed."

⁶ And Pilate commanded the whole crowd to go out, except for the twelve men who said that he was not born of fornication, and he commanded Jesus to be set apart. And Pilate said to them, "Why do they want to put him to death?" They said to Pilate, "ₗThey are in a rageₗ ˣ because he healed on the Sabbath day." Pilate said, "For a good work they want to put him to death?" They said to him, "Yes."

³·¹ And Pilate was filled with indignation and went out of the judgment hall and said to them, "I call the sun to witness that I find no fault in this man." The Jews answered and said to the governor, "If this man were not an evildoer we would not have delivered him over to you."ʸ And Pilate said, "You take him and judge him according to your law." The Jews said to Pilate, "It is not lawful for us to put anyone to death."ᶻ Pilate said, "Has God forbidden you to kill, but *allowed* me?"

² And Pilate again went into the judgment hall and called Jesus apart and said to him, "Are you the King of the Jews?" Jesus answered Pilate, "Do you say this thing yourself, or did others say *this* to you about me?" Pilate answered to Jesus, "Am I also a Jew? Your own people and the chief priests have delivered you over to me. What have you done?" Jesus answered, "My kingdom is not of this world; for if my kingdom were of this world, my servants would have fought that I would not be delivered to the Jews. But now my kingdom is not from here." Pilate said to him, "Are you a king, then?" Jesus answered him, "You say that I am a king; for this reason I was born

---

x. Literally "They have jealousy"
y. John 18:30
z. John 18:31

and have come, that everyone who is of the truth should hear my voice." Pilate said to him, "What is truth?"[aa] Jesus said to him, "Truth is of heaven." Pilate said, "Is there no truth on earth?" Jesus said to Pilate, "You see how those who speak the truth are judged by those who have authority on earth."

[4.1] And leaving Jesus in the judgment hall, Pilate went out to the Jews and said to them, "I find no fault in him."[ab] The Jews said to him, "This one said, 'I am able to destroy this temple and build it up in three days.' "[ac] Pilate said, "What temple?" The Jews said, "The one that Solomon built in forty-six years, but this one says he will destroy and build it in three days." Pilate said to them, "I am innocent of the blood of this righteous man. You see to it." The Jews said, "His blood be upon us and on our children."[ad]

[2] And Pilate called the elders and the priests and Levites to him and said to them secretly, "Do not do this, for there is nothing that you have accused him of that is worthy of death, for your accusation regards healing and profaning of the Sabbath." The elders and the priests and Levites said, "If someone blasphemes against Caesar, is he worthy of death or not?" Pilate said, "He is worthy of death." The Jews said to Pilate, "Someone is worthy of death if he blasphemes against Caesar, but this man has blasphemed against God."

[3] Then the governor commanded all the Jews to go out from the judgment hall, and calling Jesus, he said to him, "What should I do with you?" Jesus said to Pilate, "As it has been given to you." Pilate said, "How has it been given?" Jesus said, "Moses and the prophets foretold my death and resurrection." Now the Jews inquired sneakily and upon hearing they said to Pilate, "What more do you need to hear of this blasphemy?" Pilate said to the Jews, "If this word is blasphemy, you take him for his blasphemy, and bring him into your synagogue and judge him according to your law."[ae] The Jews said to Pilate, "It is contained in our law, that if a man sin against a

---

aa. John 18:33–39
ab. John 18:38
ac. Matt 26:61; Mark 14:58
ad. Matt 27:24–26
ae. John 18:31

man, he is worthy to receive forty stripes save one, but he who blasphemes against God, that ₁he will surely be stoned₁."[af]

4 Pilate said to them, "You take him and punish him however you want." The Jews said to Pilate, "We want him to be crucified." Pilate said, "He does not deserve to be crucified."

5 Now as the governor looked round about upon the crowd of Jews who stood by, he saw many of the Jews weeping, and said, "Not all the crowd wants him to be put to death." The elders of the Jews said, "For this reason our whole crowd has come here, that he should be put to death." Pilate said to the Jews, "Why should he die?" The Jews said, "Because he called himself the Son of God, and a king."[ag]

5.1 But Nicodemus, a certain Jewish man, stood before the governor and said, "I urge you, pious one, call upon me to speak a few words." Pilate said, "Speak." Nicodemus said, "I said to the elders and the priests and Levites and to all the multitude of the Jews in the synagogue, 'What do you seek with this man? This man does many signs and wonders, which no one has done or will do. Leave him alone and do not wish any evil against him. If the signs that he does are of God, they will stand, but if they are of men, they will come to nothing.[ah] For even Moses, upon being sent from God into Egypt, did many signs, which God told him to do before Pharaoh, king of Egypt. And there were men there, servants of Pharaoh, Jannes and Jambres, and they also did signs, not a few of which Moses did, and the Egyptians held them as gods, Jannes and Jambres. And since the signs that they did were not of God, they were destroyed; they and those who believed them. And now let this man go, for he is not worthy of death.'"

2 The Jews said to Nicodemus, "You became his disciple and ₁spoke₁[ai] on his behalf." Nicodemus said to them, "And has the governor also become

---

af. Literally "he should be stoned with stoning"
ag. John 19:7
ah. Acts 5:38–39
ai. Literally "made words"

his disciple, that ₍he speaks₎[aj] on his behalf? Did not Caesar appoint him to this worthiness?" And the Jews were raging and gnashing their teeth against Nicodemus. Pilate said to them, "Why do you gnash your teeth against him upon hearing the truth?" The Jews said to Nicodemus, "May you receive his truth and his ₍fate₎."[ak] Nicodemus said, "Amen, Amen. May I receive it as you have said."

6.1 Now approaching hastily, one of the Jews asked the governor to speak a word. The governor said, "If you want to say something, speak." And the Jew said, "I, for thirty-eight years, lay on a bed in in great anguish. And when Jesus came, many of the demon-possessed and those ₍incapacitated₎[al] by various diseases were healed by him. And certain young men took pity on me and carried me with my bed and brought me to him; and when Jesus saw me he had compassion, and spoke a word to me, 'Take up your bed and walk.' And I took up my bed and walked."[am] The Jews said to Pilate, "Ask him what day it was upon which he was healed?" He who was healed said, "On the Sabbath." The Jews said, "Did we not teach this, that on the Sabbath he healed and cast out demons?"

2 And approaching hastily, another Jew said, "I was born blind. I would hear a voice but not see a face. And as Jesus passed by I cried with a loud voice, 'Have mercy on me, O son of David!' And he took pity on me and put his hands on my eyes and I received sight immediately."[an]

And approaching hastily, another Jew said, "₍I had a crooked spine₎[ao] and he made me straight with a word." And another said, "I was a leper, and he healed me with a word."

7.1 And a certain woman named Bernice, crying out from far away, said, "I had a flow of blood and I touched the hem of his garment, and the flow of

---

aj. Literally "he makes words"
ak. Literally "portion"
al. Literally "laid down"
am. Matt 9:1–8; Mark 2:1–12; Luke 5:17–26; John 5:1–13
an. Matt 20:29–34; Mark 10:46–52; Luke 18:35–43
ao. Literally "I was bowed"

my blood, which *I had* for twelve years, stopped."[ap] The Jews said, "We have a law not to permit a woman to give testimony."

8.1 And others, even a crowd of both men and women, cried out, saying, "This man is a prophet and the demons are subject to him." Pilate said to those who said the demons are subject to him, "Why are your teachers not also subject to him?" They said to Pilate, "We do not know." And others said that he raised up Lazarus, who was dead, out of his tomb after four days. And beginning to tremble, the governor said to the whole crowd of the Jews, "Why do you want to spill innocent blood?"

9.1 And calling Nicodemus and the twelve men who said that he was not born of fornication, he said to them, "What shall I do? A riot is starting among the people." They said to him, "We do not know; let them see to it." Pilate, again calling for the whole crowd of the Jews, said, "You know that you have a custom to release to you one prisoner at the feast of unleavened bread. I have one in prison under condemnation, a murderer named Barabbas, and this Jesus who also stands before you, in whom I find no fault. Whom do you wish that I release unto you?" And they cried out, "Barabbas!" Pilate said, "Then what shall I do with Jesus who is called Christ?" The Jews said, "Let him be crucified."[aq] But some of the Jews answered, "You are not a friend of Caesar's if you let this man go;[ar] for he called himself the Son of God and a king. Therefore you want him for king and not Caesar."

2 And becoming angry, Pilate said to the Jews, "Your nation is always seditious and you rebel against your benefactors." The Jews said, "Against what benefactors?" Pilate said, "As I have heard, your God brought you out of Egypt, out of hard slavery, and led you safe through the sea as if by dry land. And in the wilderness he nourished you with manna and gave you quails, and gave you water to drink out of a rock, and gave to you a law. And in all these things you provoked your God to anger, and sought out a molten calf, and angered your God. And he sought to kill you. And Moses made

---

ap. Matt 9:20–22; Mark 5:25–34; Luke 8:43–48
aq. Matt 27:15–23; Mark 15:6–15; Luke 23:18–25; John 18:39–40
ar. John 19:23

supplication for you and you were not put to death. And now you accuse me that I hate the king." ³ And getting up from the judgment seat, he wanted to go out. And the Jews cried out, saying, "We know our king, Caesar and not Jesus. For even the wise men from the east brought gifts to him as to a king. And Herod, upon hearing from the wise men that a king was born, sought to kill him. But knowing *this*, his father Joseph took him and his mother and they fled into Egypt. And upon hearing *it*, Herod destroyed the children of the Hebrews that were born in Bethlehem."[as]

⁴ And upon hearing these words, Pilate was afraid. And upon silencing the multitude, because they were crying out, Pilate said to them, "So, then, this is the one whom Herod sought?" The Jews said, "Yes, this is the one." And Pilate took water and washed his hands before the sun, saying, "I am innocent of the blood of this righteous one. You see to it." Again the Jews cried out, "His blood be upon us and upon our children."[at]

⁵ Then Pilate commanded the veil to be drawn before the judgment seat upon which he sat, and said to Jesus, "Your nation has convicted you as a king. For this reason I have decreed that you should first be flogged according to the law of the pious kings, and then hung upon the cross in the garden where you were captured. And let the two criminals Dysmas and Gestas be crucified with you."

¹⁰·¹ And Jesus went out of the judgment hall, and the two criminals with him. And when they came to the place, they stripped him of his garments and clothed him with a linen cloth and put a crown of thorns around his head. In the same way they also hung up the two criminals. But Jesus said, "Father, forgive them, for they do not know what they do." And the soldiers divided his garments among them.[au] And the people stood looking at him. And ridiculing him, the chief priests and the rulers with them said, "He saved others; let him save himself. If he is the Son of God, let him come down from the cross." And the soldiers mocked him, coming and offering

---

as. Matt 2:7–18
at. Matt 27:24–26
au. Luke 23:34

him vinegar with gall. And they said, "If you are the King of the Jews, save yourself!"[av] And Pilate after the sentence ordered his accusation be written as a title in letters of Greek and Latin and Hebrew, according to the saying of the Jews, that he was the King of the Jews.

2 And one of the criminals that was hanged[aw] spoke to him, saying, "If you are the Christ, save yourself and us." But answering, Dysmas rebuked him, saying, "Do you not fear God at all, seeing you are in the same judgment? And we indeed justly *deserve it*, for we receive the due reward of our actions; but this man has done nothing wrong." And he said to Jesus, "Remember me, Lord, in your kingdom." And Jesus said to him, "Truly, truly I say to you, that today you will be with me in paradise."[ax]

11.1 And it was about the sixth hour, and there was darkness over the land until the ninth hour, as the sun was darkened. And the veil of the temple was ripped in two. And calling with a loud voice, Jesus said, "Father, *badd ach ephkid rouel*," which is interpreted, "Into your hands I commit my spirit." And having said this, he gave up his spirit. And upon seeing what had happened, the centurion glorified God, saying, "This man was righteous." And the whole crowd that had come to this sight, upon seeing what had happened, beat their breasts and turned away.[ay]

2 But the centurion reported to the governor the things that had happened. And when the governor and his wife heard, they were greatly grieved, and did not eat or drink on that day. And Pilate sent for the Jews and said to them, "Did you see what happened?" But they said, "There was a naturally occurring eclipse of the sun."

3 And his[az] acquaintances and the women who came with him from Galilee stood far away, watching these things. But a certain man named Joseph, a counselor of the city of Arimathea, who also himself looked for the

---

av. Matt 27:38–43; Mark 15:27–32; Luke 23:35–38
aw. Gestas, see §9.5 above
ax. Luke 23:39–43
ay. Luke 23:44–48
az. That is, Jesus'

kingdom of God, this man went to Pilate and asked for the body of Jesus. And he took it down and wrapped it in a clean linen cloth and laid it in a tomb hewn from stone in which no one ever had yet been laid.[ba]

12.1 And the Jews, upon hearing that Joseph had asked for the body of Jesus, looked for him and for the twelve men who said that Jesus was not born of fornication, and for Nicodemus and many others who had come before Pilate and declared his good works. But they all hid themselves, and only Nicodemus was seen by them, because he was a ruler of the Jews. And Nicodemus said to them, "How did you come into the synagogue?" The Jews said to him, "How did you come into the synagogue? Because you are a conspirator with him, and his portion will be yours in the life to come." Nicodemus said, "Amen, amen." Likewise even Joseph, coming forward, said to them, "Why is it that you are angry with me because I asked for the body of Jesus? Look, I have laid it in my new tomb, having wrapped it in clean linen, and I rolled a stone over the door of the cave. And you have not dealt well with the righteous one because you did not repent after you crucified him, but you also pierced him with a spear."

But the Jews took hold of Joseph, commanding him to be secured until the first day of the week. And they said to him, "You know that the hour does not allow us to do anything against you, because the Sabbath dawns. But know that you will not obtain burial, but we will give your flesh to the birds of the sky." Joseph said to them, "This boastful word is like Goliath who reproached the living God and the holy David. For God said by the prophet, 'Vengeance is mine and I will repay, says the Lord.'[bb] And now, behold, one who was uncircumcised, but circumcised in heart, took water and washed his hands before the sun, saying, 'I am innocent of the blood of this righteous person. You see to it.' And answering Pilate, you said, 'His blood be upon us and upon our children.'[bc] And now I fear lest the wrath of the Lord come upon you and upon your children, as you have said." But upon hearing these words the Jews were embittered in soul. And catching hold

---

ba. Matt 27:57–61; Mark 15:42–46; Luke 23:50–53; John 19:38–42
bb. Rom 12:19 citing Deut 32:35
bc. Matt 27:24–26

of Joseph they took him and secured him in a house with no window, and guards were set at the door. And they sealed the door of the place where Joseph was secured.

² And on the Sabbath day the rulers of the synagogue and the priests and the Levites ₁established a rule₁ᵇᵈ that everyone should appear in the synagogue on the first day of the week. And rising early, the whole crowd took counsel in the synagogue ₁to determine how₁ᵇᵉ they should kill him. And upon being seated, the council commanded him to be brought in with great shame. And upon opening the door they did not find him. And all the people were amazed, and they became astonished because they found the seals closed, and Caiaphas had the key. And they no longer dared to lay hands upon those who had spoken on behalf of Jesus before Pilate.

¹³·¹ And while still seated in the synagogue and astonished because of Joseph, there came some of the guard that the Jews had asked Pilate to keep the tomb of Jesus, lest his disciples should come and steal him away. And they reported, saying to the rulers of the synagogue and the priests and the Levites what had happened: "Somehow there was a great earthquake, and we saw an angel descend from heaven, and he rolled away the stone from the mouth of the cave, and sat upon it. And he was shining like snow and like lightning, and we were very afraid and ₁pretended to be dead₁.ᵇᶠᵇᵍ And we heard the voice of the angel speaking with the women who waited at the tomb: "Do not fear, for I know that you seek Jesus who was crucified. He is not here, he is risen, as he said. Come, see the place where the Lord lay. Now go quickly, tell his disciples that he is risen from the dead, and is in Galilee."ᵇʰ

² The Jews said, "Which women did he speak with?" Those of the guard said, "We do not know who they were." The Jews said, "What hour was it?" Those of the guard said, "Midnight." The Jews said, "And why did you

---

bd. Literally "set a boundary"
be. Literally "by what death"
bf. Literally "lay as dead people"
bg. Matt 28:2–4
bh. Matt 28:5–7

not take the women?" Those of the guard said, "We became like dead men through fear, and we did not look to see the light of the day; how then could we take them?" The Jews said, "As the Lord lives, we do not believe you." Those of the guard said to the Jews, "You saw so many signs in that man, and you did not believe, how then should you believe us? Truly you swore rightly 'as the Lord lives,' for he does live." Again those of the guard said, "We have heard *the reports* of the one who asked for the body of Jesus, that you secured him and that you sealed the door; and when you opened it you did not find him. So you give *us* Joseph and we will give you Jesus." The Jews said, "Joseph has departed to his own city." Those of the guard said to the Jews, "And Jesus is risen, as we have heard from the angel, and he is in Galilee."

³ And the Jews, upon hearing these words, were exceedingly fearful, saying, "*Take heed* lest this report be heard and everyone ₍starts to listen to₎[bi] Jesus." And the Jews took counsel and laid down a large sum of money and gave it to the soldiers, saying, "You say: 'While we slept his disciples came by night and stole him away.' And if this comes to the governor's hearing we will persuade him and secure you."[bj] And they took *it* and did as they were instructed.

¹⁴·¹ Now a certain priest, Phineas, and a teacher, Addas, and a Levite, Aggaeus, came down from Galilee to Jerusalem and told the rulers of the synagogue and the priests and the Levites: "We saw Jesus and his disciples sitting upon the mountain that is called Mamilch, and he said to his disciples, 'Go into all the world and preach to the whole creation: The one who believes and is baptized will be saved, but the one who does not believe will be condemned. And these signs will follow those who believe: In my name they will cast out demons, they will speak with new tongues, they will take up snakes, and if they drink any deadly thing it will not hurt them. They will lay hands upon the sick and the sick will recover.'[bk] And while Jesus was still speaking to his disciples we saw him taken up into heaven."

---

bi. Literally "incline to"
bj. Matt 28:12–14
bk. Mark 16:15–18

² The elders and the priests and Levites said, "Give glory to the God of Israel and make confession to him: Did you actually hear and see those things that you have told us?" Those who told them said, "As the Lord God of our fathers Abraham, Isaac, and Jacob lives, we did hear these things and we saw him taken up into heaven." The elders and the priests and the Levites said to them, "Did you come for this reason, that you might tell us, or did you come to pay your vows to God?" And they said, "To pay our vows to God." The elders and the chief priests and the Levites said to them, "If you came to pay your vows to God, what is the purpose of this idle tale that you have babbled before all the people?" Phineas the priest and Addas the teacher and Aggaeus the Levite said to the rulers of the synagogue and priests and Levites, "If these words that we have spoken and seen are sin, behold, we are before you. Do to us what seems good in your eyes." And they took the law and adjured them *by it* that they should no longer tell anyone these words. And they gave them food and drink, and put them out of the city. Moreover they gave them money, and three men to go with them, and they set them on their way as far as Galilee, and they departed in peace.

³ Now when these men had departed to Galilee, the chief priests and the rulers of the synagogue and the elders gathered together in the synagogue, and shut the gate, and mourned with great mourning, saying, "What is this sign that has come to pass in Israel?" But Annas and Caiaphas said, "Why are you troubled? Why do you weep? Do you not know that his disciples gave a large amount of gold to those who kept the tomb and taught them to say that an angel came down and rolled away the stone from the door of the tomb?" But the priests and the elders said, "₁We wish it were true₁bl that his disciples stole away his body; but how is his soul entered into his body, and how does he live in Galilee?" Now they could not answer these things, and in the end said with difficulty, "It is not lawful for us to believe the uncircumcised."

¹⁵·¹ And Nicodemus got up and stood before the council, saying, "What you say is right. Do you not know, O people of the Lord, the men who came down out of Galilee, that they fear God and are men of substance, hating

---

bl. Literally "be it so"

covetousness, men of peace? And they have told you with an oath, 'We saw Jesus upon the mountain Mamilch with his disciples and he taught them all things that you heard of them, and we saw him taken up into heaven.' And no one asked them in what manner he was taken up. For it is just like the book of the holy Scriptures has taught us, that Elijah was also taken up into heaven, and Elisha cried out with a loud voice, and Elijah threw his hairy cloak upon Elisha, and Elisha cast the cloak upon the Jordan and passed over and went to Jericho. And the sons of the prophets met him and said, 'Elisha, where is your master Elijah?' And he said that he was taken up into heaven. And they said to Elisha, 'Perhaps a spirit caught him up and cast him upon one of the mountains? But let us take our servants with us and look for him.' And they persuaded Elisha and he went with them, and they looked for him for three days and did not find him.[bm] And they knew that he had been taken up. And now listen to me, and let us send to all the boundaries of Israel and see whether the Christ was not taken up by a spirit and cast upon one of the mountains." And this saying pleased them all: and they sent into all the boundaries and looked for Jesus and did not find him. But they found Joseph in Arimathea, and no man dared to lay hands upon him.

² And they told the elders and the priests and the Levites, "We went throughout all the boundaries of Israel, and we did not find Jesus; but we did find Joseph in Arimathea."

And upon hearing about Joseph they rejoiced and gave glory to the God of Israel. And the rulers of the synagogue and the priests and the Levites took counsel how they should meet with Joseph, and they took a roll of papyrus and wrote to Joseph these words:

"Peace to you. We know that we have sinned against God and against you, and we have prayed to the God of Israel that you would consider it a worthy thing to come to your ancestors[bn] and to your children, for we are all troubled because when we opened the door we did not find you and we know

bm. Kgs 2:1–18
bn. Or "fathers"

that we concocted an evil scheme against you, but the Lord helped you. And the Lord himself made our scheme of no effect against you, O father Joseph, you who are honorable among all the people."

3 And they chose out of all Israel seven men who were friends of Joseph, whom Joseph himself also accounted his friends, and the rulers of the synagogue and the priests and the Levites said to them, "See to it. If upon receiving our letter he reads it, know that he will come with you to us. But if he does not read it, know that he is angry with us, so you greet him in peace and return to us." And they blessed the men and let them go.

And the men came to Joseph and bowed down before him, and said to him, "Peace be to you." And he said, "Peace be to you and to all the people of Israel." And they gave him the book of the letter, and upon receiving it Joseph read and embraced the letter. And he blessed God and said, "Blessed be the Lord God, who has redeemed Israel from shedding innocent blood; and blessed be the Lord, who sent his angel and sheltered me under his wings." And he prepared a meal,[bo] for them, and they ate and drank and slept there.

4 And rising early in the morning, they prayed. And Joseph saddled his donkey and went with the men, and they came to the holy city Jerusalem. And all the people came to Joseph and cried out, "Peace be to your arrival!" And he said to all the people, "Peace be to you." And all the people kissed him. And the people prayed with Joseph, and they were astonished at seeing him.

And Nicodemus welcomed him into his house and made a great feast, and called Annas and Caiaphas and the elders and the priests and the Levites to his house. And they celebrated, eating and drinking with Joseph. And after singing a hymn, each one went to his house. But Joseph remained in the house of Nicodemus.

5 And on the next day, which was the day of preparation, the rulers of the synagogue and the priests and the Levites rose up early and came to the house of Nicodemus, and Nicodemus met them and said, "Peace be to you."

---

bo. Literally "he set a table"

And they said, "Peace be to you and to Joseph and to all your house and to all the house of Joseph." And he brought them into his house. And the whole council was set, and Joseph sat between Annas and Caiaphas; and no man dared speak a word to him. And Joseph said, "Why is it that you have called me?" And they motioned to Nicodemus that he should speak to Joseph. And opening his mouth, Nicodemus said to Joseph, "Father, you know that the honored teachers and the priests and the Levites desire to learn a word from you." And Joseph said, "You may ask." And taking *the book of* the law, Annas and Caiaphas adjured Joseph, saying, "Give glory to the God of Israel and make confession to him. For Achan,[bp] when he was adjured by the prophet Joshua, did not commit perjury but declared to him all things, and did not hide a word from him. Therefore you also do not hide from us so much as a word." And Joseph *said*, "I will not hide one word from you." And they said to him, "We were greatly angered because you asked for the body of Jesus and wrapped it in a clean linen cloth and laid him in a tomb. And for this reason we put you securely in a house that had no window, and we put keys and seals upon the doors, and guards guarded the place where you were secured. And on the first day of the week we opened it and did not find you, and we were greatly troubled, and wonder fell upon all the people of the Lord until yesterday. Now, therefore, tell us what happened to you."

[6] And Joseph said, "On the day of preparation, at about the tenth hour, you secured me, and I continued there the whole Sabbath. And at midnight as I stood and prayed the house where you secured me was taken up by the four corners, and I saw ⌊something like⌋[bq] a flashing of light in my eyes. And being filled with fear I fell to the ground. And someone took me by the hand and removed me from the place where I had fallen; and a mist of water was shed *on me* from my head to my feet, and an odor of myrrh came about my ⌊nose⌋.[br] And wiping my face he kissed me and said to me, "Fear not, Joseph. Open your eyes and see who it is that speaks with you." And looking up, I saw Jesus. And I began to tremble, thinking it was a ghost.

---

bp. Gk. *Achar*
bq. Literally "as it were"
br. Literally "nostrils"

And I said the commandments, and he said them with me. And as you are
not ignorant that a spirit, if it meet any man and hear the commandments,
it immediately flees. And seeing that he said them with me, I said to him,
"Rabbi Elijah?" And he said to me, "I am not Elijah." And I said to him, "Who
are you, Lord?" And he said to me, "I am Jesus, whose body you asked for
from Pilate. And you clothed me in clean linen and covered my face with
a napkin, and laid me in your new cave, and rolled a great stone upon the
door of the cave." And I said to him who spoke with me, "Show me the place
where I laid you." And he brought me and showed me the place where I laid
him, and the linen cloth laid inside, and the napkin that was upon his face.
And I knew that it was Jesus. And he took me by the hand and set me in the
middle of my house, the doors being shut, and laid me upon my bed and
said to me, "Peace be to you." And he kissed me and said to me, "Do not go
out of your house for forty days, for behold, I go to my brothers in Galilee."

16.1 And upon hearing these words of Joseph, the rulers of the synagogue and
the priests and the Levites became as dead men and fell to the ground and
fasted until the ninth hour. And Nicodemus with Joseph comforted Annas
and Caiaphas and the priests and the Levites, saying, "Get up and stand on
your feet and taste bread and strengthen your souls, because tomorrow is
the Sabbath of the Lord." And they got up and prayed to God and ate and
drank, and each man departed to his house.

2 And on the Sabbath our teachers and the priests and Levites sat and questioned one another and said, "What is this wrath that is come upon us? For
we know his father and his mother." Levi the teacher said, "I know that his
parents fear God and do not hold back their prayers and pay tithes three
times a year. And when Jesus was born, his parents brought him up to this
place and gave sacrifices and burnt offerings to God. And when the great
teacher Simeon took him into his arms and said: "Now let your servant,
Lord, depart in peace, for my eyes have seen your salvation, which you
have prepared before the face of all peoples, a light to lighten the Gentiles
and the glory of your people Israel." And Simeon blessed them and said to
Mary his mother, "I give you good news concerning this child." And Mary
said, "Good, my lord?" And Simeon said to her, "Yes, good. Behold, he is
appointed for the fall and rising again of many in Israel, and for a sign

that is spoken against. And a sword will pierce through your own heart also, that the thoughts of many hearts may be revealed."[bs]

3 They said to Levi the teacher, "How do you know these things?" Levi said to them, "Do you not know that I learned the law from him?" The council said to him, "We want to see your father." And they sent for his father, and questioned him, and he said to them, "Why did you not believe my son? The blessed and righteous Simeon, he taught him the law." The council said, "Rabbi Levi, is the word true that you spoke?" And he said, "It is true."

Then the rulers of the synagogue and the priests and the Levites said among themselves, "Come, let us send into Galilee for the three men who came and told us of his teaching and his ascension, and let them tell us how they saw him taken up." And this word pleased them all, and they sent the three men who before had gone with them into Galilee and said to them, "Say to Rabbi Addas and Rabbi Phineas and Rabbi Aggaeus, 'Peace be to you and to all who are with you. Since great questioning has come about in the council, we have sent to you to call you to this holy place of Jerusalem.'"

4 And the men went into Galilee and found them sitting and meditating upon the law, and greeted them in peace. And the men who were in Galilee said to those who came to them, "Peace be upon all Israel." And they said, "Peace be to you." Again they said to them, "Why have you come?" And they who were sent said, "The council calls you to the holy city Jerusalem." And when the men heard that they were summoned by the council, they prayed to God and reclined for a meal with the men and ate and drank. And they got up and came in peace to Jerusalem.

5 And on the next day the council was set in the synagogue, and they questioned them, saying, "Did you really see Jesus sitting on the mountain Mamilch as he taught his eleven disciples, and you saw him taken up?" And the men answered them and said, "Just as we saw him taken up, so we told it to you."

---

bs. Luke 2:28–35

⁶ Annas said, "ₗSeparate them₎,bt and let us see if their word agrees." And ₗthey separated them₎.bu And they called Addas first and said to him, "How did you see Jesus taken up?" Addas said, "While he still sat upon the mountain Mamilch and taught his disciples, we saw a cloud that overshadowed him and his disciples. And the cloud carried him up into heaven, and his disciples were laying with their faces upon the earth." And they called Phineas the priest, and also questioned him, saying, "How did you see Jesus taken up?" And he spoke likewise. And again they asked Aggacus, and he also spoke likewise. And the council said, "It is contained in the law of Moses, 'At the mouth of two or three every word will be established.' "bv

Bouthem the teacher said, "It is written in the law, 'Enoch walked with God and is not, because God took him.' "bw Jaeirus the teacher said, "And we have heard of the death of the holy Moses, and have not seen him; for it is written in the law of the Lord, 'And Moses died at the mouth of the Lord, and no man knew of his tomb to this day.' "bx And Rabbi Levi said, "Why was it that Rabbi Simeon said when he saw Jesus, 'Behold, this one is set for the fall and rising again of many in Israel, and for a sign spoken against?' "by And Rabbi Isaac said, "It is written in the law, 'Behold I send my messenger before your face, who will go before you to keep you in every good way, for my name is named thereon.' "bz

⁷ Then Annas and Caiaphas said, "You have spoken well those things that are written in the law of Moses, that no man saw the death of Enoch, and no one has named the death of Moses. But *we know that* Jesus spoke before Pilate, and that we saw him receive blows and spit upon his face, and that the soldiers put a crown of thorns on him, and that he was whipped and condemned by Pilate, and that he was crucified at *the place of* the skull and two thieves with him, and that they gave him vinegar to drink with gall, and that Longinus the soldier pierced his side with a spear, and that

---

bt. Literally "set them apart one from another"
bu. Literally "they set them apart one from another"
bv. Deut 19:15
bw. Gen 5:24
bx. Deut 34:5–6
by. Luke 2:34
bz. Exod 23:20–21

Joseph our honorable father asked for his body, and that, as he said, he rose again, and as the three teachers say, 'We saw him taken up into heaven,' and that Rabbi Levi spoke, testifying to the things which were spoken by Rabbi Simeon, and that he said, 'Behold this one is set for the fall and rising again of many in Israel and for a sign spoken against.' "[ca]

And all the teachers said to all the people of the Lord, "If this has come to pass from the Lord, and it is marvelous in our eyes, you will surely know, O house of Jacob, that it is written, 'Cursed is every one that hangs upon a tree.'[cb] And another scripture teaches, 'The gods who did not make the heaven and the earth will perish.' "[cc]

And the priests and the Levites said one to another, "If ₗhe is rememberedⱼ[cd] until the year[ce] which is called Jubilee,[cf] know that he will prevail forever and will raise up for himself a new people."

Then the rulers of the synagogue and the priests and the Levites admonished all Israel, saying, "Cursed is that man who worships what was made by a human hand, and cursed is the man who worships what is created alongside the Creator." And all the people said, "Amen, Amen."

[8] And all the people sang a hymn to the Lord and said, "Blessed be the Lord who has given rest to the people of Israel according to all that he spoke. Not one word has fallen to the ground of all his good sayings that he spoke to his servant Moses. The Lord our God be with us as he was with our ancestors.[cg] Let him not destroy us. And let him not destroy us from turning our heart unto him, from walking in all his ways and keeping his statutes and his judgments that he commanded our fathers. And the Lord will be King over all the earth in that day. And there will be one Lord and his name one, even the Lord our King. He will save us. There is none like you, O Lord. You

---

ca. Luke 2:34
cb. Deut 21:23
cc. Jer 10:11
cd. Literally "his remembrance"
ce. Gk. *Sōmmou*, Ehrman and Pleše note this may be a corruption of the Hebrew for "year"
cf. Gk. *Iōbēl*
cg. Or "fathers"

are great, O Lord, and great is your name. Heal us, O Lord, by your power, and we will be healed. Save us, Lord, and we will be saved, for we are your portion and your inheritance. And the Lord will not forsake his people for his great name's sake, for the Lord has begun to make us to be his people."

And upon singing the hymn, they all departed, each man to his house, glorifying God, for his is the glory, ₁forever and ever₁.ᶜʰ Amen.

DESCENT OF CHRIST INTO HADES

1.1 Joseph said, "And why do you marvel that Jesus rose again? This is not marvelous. But this is marvelous, that he did not rise alone, but raised up many other dead people who appeared to many in Jerusalem. And if you do not know the others, *there is* at least Simeon, who received Jesus, and his two sons, whom he raised up; these at least you know. For we buried them only a short time ago, and now their tombs are seen to be opened and empty, and they themselves are alive and dwelling in Arimathea." Therefore they sent men, and found their tombs opened and empty. Joseph said, "Let us go to Arimathea and find them."

2 Then the chief priests Annas and Caiaphas rose up, and Joseph and Nicodemus and Gamaliel and others with them, and they went to Arimathea and found the men of whom Joseph spoke. So they offered prayer, and greeted one another. Then they came with them to Jerusalem; and they brought them into the synagogue and fastened the doors shut, and set the ancient *book* of the Jews in the midst. And the high priests said to them, "We want you to swear an oath by the God of Israel and by Adonai, and so speak the truth, how you arose and who raised you from the dead."

3 Upon hearing this, those who had arisen made on their faces the sign of the cross, and said to the chief priests, "Give us paper and ink and pen." So they brought these things. And they sat down and wrote as follows:

2.1 "O Lord Jesus Christ, the resurrection and the life of the world, give us grace that we may tell of your resurrection and of your marvelous works

---

ch. Literally "to the ages of the ages"

that you did in Hades. We, then, were in Hades together with all those who had fallen asleep since the beginning. And at the hour of midnight there rose upon those dark places as it were the light of the sun, and it shined, and we all were enlightened and saw one another. And immediately our father Abraham, together with the patriarchs and the prophets, were all at once filled with joy and said to one another, 'This light is from the great illumination.' The prophet Isaiah who was there said, 'This light is of the Father, and of the Son, and of the Holy Ghost; concerning which I prophesied when I was yet alive, saying, "The land of Zebulon and the land of Naphtali,[ci] the people who sat in darkness, have seen a great light." ' "[cj]

² "Then there came into the midst another out of the wilderness, an ascetic, and the patriarchs said to him, 'Who are you?' And he said, 'I am John, the last of the prophets, who made straight the ways of the Son of God, and preached repentance to the people for the remission of sins. And the Son of God came to me, and when I saw him a ways off I said to the people, "Behold the Lamb of God who takes away the sins of the world."[ck] And with my hands I baptized him in the river Jordan, and saw as it were a dove, and the Holy Ghost coming upon him, and I also heard the voice of God and the Father speaking in this way: "This is my beloved Son, in whom I am well pleased."[cl] And for this reason he also sent me to you, to proclaim that the only begotten Son of God has come, that whoever believes on him may be saved,[cm] and whoever does not believe on him may be condemned. Therefore I say to all of you, that when you see him you will worship him, for now is only the time of repentance for you, because you worshiped idols in the vain world that is above, and for the sins that you committed. But at another time it is impossible that this should come to pass.' "

³·¹ "And as John was in this way teaching those who were in Hades, the first-created Adam, the first father, also heard it, and said to Seth his son,

---

ci. Gk. *Nephthaleim*
cj. Isa 9:1–2
ck. John 1:29
cl. Matt 3:16–17
cm. John 3:16

'My son, I want you to tell the ancestors[cn] of the race of men, and the prophets; when I fell ₗand was near death,ᵢ[co] where I sent you.' And Seth said, 'You prophets and patriarchs, listen. My father Adam, the first-created, when he fell ₗand was near death,ᵢ[cp] sent me to make supplication to God by the gate of paradise, that he would lead me by his angel to the tree of mercy, and I should take the oil and anoint my father, and he should arise from his sickness. This I also did, and after my prayer an angel of the Lord came and said to me, "What do you ask, Seth? Are you asking for the oil that raises up the sick, or for the tree that flows with that oil, for the sickness of your father? This cannot be found now. So go and say to your father that after the completion of five thousand five hundred years from the creation of the world, then the only-begotten Son of God will become man and come down upon the earth, and he will anoint him with that oil, and he will arise. And with water and the Holy Ghost he will wash him and those who come of him. And then he will be healed of every disease, but now it is impossible that this should happen." ' And when the patriarchs and prophets heard these things, they rejoiced greatly."

4.1 "And while all of them were so joyful, Satan the heir of darkness came and said to Hades, 'O you who devours all and is insatiable, listen to my words. There is one of the race of the Jews, Jesus, who calls himself the Son of God, but this one is a man, and by our working together the Jews have crucified him. And now that he has died, you be prepared that we may secure him here. For I know that he is a man, and I have heard him saying, "My soul is exceedingly sorrowful, even to death."[cq] And he has done much hurt to me in the world that is above while he walked among men. For wherever he found my servants he persecuted them, and as many as I caused to be injured, or blind, or lame, or leprous, or any such thing, he healed them with only a word. And when I prepared many to be buried, he also restored them again with only a word.' "

---

cn. Or "forefathers"
co. Literally "I die"
cp. Literally "he died"
cq. Matt 26:38

² "Hades said, 'And is this one so mighty that he can do such things with a word only? Or, if he is such, are you able to withstand him? It seems to me no one will be able to withstand him, but when you say that you have heard him fearing death, he said this to mock and laugh at you, willing to seize you with a mighty hand. And woe, woe to you for all the ages!' Satan said, 'O Hades that devours all and is insatiable, do you fear so much at what you have heard concerning our common adversary? I did not fear him, but I did set on the Jews, and they crucified him and also gave him gall to drink mingled with vinegar. So prepare yourself, so that when he comes you may secure him.' "

³ "Hades answered, 'O inheritor of darkness, son of perdition, devil, you said to me just now that many of those whom you prepared to be buried he restored again with only a word. Now if he had set many free from burial, how and by what strength shall he be held by us? Indeed, I recently swallowed up a certain dead man named Lazarus, and after a short time, one of the living by force snatched him up out of my entrails with only a word, and I think this is he of whom you speak. If, then, we receive him here, I fear lest we be at risk for the rest also; for I have swallowed up everyone from the beginning. Behold, I see that they are restless, and my belly causes me pain, and this Lazarus who before was snatched away from me I take to be no good sign, for he flew away from me, not like to a dead man but to an eagle, so instantly did the earth cast him out. Therefore I also implore you by your gifts and by my own, that you do not bring him to this place, for I believe that he comes here to raise up all the dead. And this I say to you: By the outer darkness, if you bring him here, not one of all the dead will be left in me.' "

⁵·¹ "And as Satan and Hades spoke in this way with one another, there came a great voice as of thunder, saying, 'Lift up, O princes, your gates, and you be lifted up, you everlasting doors, and the King of glory shall come in.'ᶜʳ When Hades heard, he said unto Satan, 'Go forth, if you are able, and withstand him.' So Satan went forth. Then Hades said to his devils, 'Fasten the brass gates well and strongly, and the bars of iron, and keep my locks, and

---

cr. Psa 23:7 (LXX)

stand upright, and beware at all points. For if he comes in here, woe will take hold on us.' "

2 "When the ancestors[cs] heard this, all of them began to insult him, saying, 'You who devoured all and who is insatiable, open up, so that the King of glory may come in.' David the prophet said, 'Do you not know, blind one, that when I lived in the world I prophesied that word, "Lift up, O princes, your gates?" '[ct] Isaiah said, 'Upon foreseeing this by the Holy Spirit, I wrote, "The dead will arise, and those who are in the tombs will awake, and those who are in the earth will rejoice"[cu] and again, "O death, where is your sting? O Hades, where is your victory?" ' "[cv]

3 "Then a voice came again, saying, 'Lift up the gates.' And when Hades heard the voice the second time, he answered as if he did not know it, and said, 'Who is this King of glory?' The angels of the Lord said, 'The Lord strong and mighty, the Lord mighty in battle.'[cw] And immediately at the word the gates of brass were broken in pieces and the bars of iron were destroyed, and all the dead who were bound were loosed from their chains, and we with them, and the King of glory entered in like a man, and all the dark places of Hades were enlightened."

6.1 "Hades immediately cried out, 'We are overcome, woe unto us. But who are you that has such great authority and power? And of what sort are you who has come here without sin? You who appear small and can do great things, who are humble and exalted, a slave and a master, a soldier and a commander, who exercises authority over the dead and the living? You were nailed to the cross, and laid in the tomb, and now you have become free and have destroyed our whole power. Are you then that Jesus, of whom the chief ruler Satan said to us that by your cross and death you would inherit the whole world?' "

---

cs. Or "forefathers"
ct. Psa 23:7 (LXX)
cu. Isa 26:19
cv. Is 25:8; 1 Cor 15:55
cw. Psa 23:8 (LXX)

2 "Then the King of glory took hold of the head of the chief ruler Satan, and delivered him to the angels and said, 'Bind down his hands and his feet and his neck and his mouth with irons.' And then he delivered him to Hades, saying, 'Take him and keep him safely until my second coming.'"

7.1 "Then Hades, when he had taken Satan, said to him, 'O Beelzebub,[cx] inheritor of fire and torment, enemy of the saints, ₁what compelled you to contrive₁[cy] that the King of glory should be crucified, so that he should come here and strip us naked? You turn and see that not one of the dead is left in me, but everything, whatever you gained by the tree of knowledge, you have lost by the tree of the cross, and all your joy is turned into sorrow, and when you would have slain the King of glory you have slain yourself. For since I have received you to keep you safely, you will learn by trial what evils I will enact upon you. O you arch-devil, the beginning of death, and root of sin, and end of all evil, what evil did you find in Jesus that you went about his destruction? How did you dare to do such great wickedness? How did you desire to bring down such a one into this darkness, through whom you are deprived of all those who have died since the beginning?'"

8.1 "And as Hades spoke in this way with Satan, the King of glory stretched out his right hand and took hold of our ancestor[cz] Adam and raised him up. And then he turned to the rest and said, 'Come with me, all of you, as many as have suffered death through the tree that this man touched. For I again raise all of you up through the tree of the cross.' And with that he put them all out. And our ancestor[da] Adam was seen full of joy. 'I give thanks to your greatness, O Lord,' he said, 'for you have brought me up out of the lowest depth of Hades.' Likewise also all the prophets and the saints said, 'We give thanks to you, O Christ, Savior of the world, because you have brought up our life from corruption.'"

2 "And when they had said these things, the Savior blessed Adam upon his forehead with the sign of the cross. And he also did this to all the patriarchs

---

cx. Gk. *Beelzeboul*
cy. Literally "what need did you have to provide"
cz. Or "forefather"
da. Or "forefather"

and prophets and martyrs and ancestors.[db] And he took them and jumped up out of Hades. And as he went the holy fathers sang praises, following him *and* saying, 'Blessed is he who comes in the name of the Lord! Hallelujah!'[dc] To him *be* the glory of all the saints.'"

9.1 "Therefore, going into paradise holding our ancestor[dd] Adam by the hand, he delivered him to Michael the archangel, along with all of the righteous. While they were entering in at the door of paradise, two elderly people greeted them, to whom the holy fathers said, 'Who are you, who have not seen death nor come down into Hades, but who dwell in paradise with your bodies and souls?' And answering one of them said, 'I am Enoch who pleased God and was translated here by him. And this is Elijah the Tishbite. And we will live until the end of the world, but at that time we will be sent by God to withstand the Antichrist and to be killed by him, and after three days to rise and be caught up in the clouds to meet the Lord.'"[de]

10.1 "While speaking these things, another humble person came, also carrying a cross upon his shoulder, to whom the holy fathers said, 'Who are you, who has the look of a robber, and what is that cross that you carry on your shoulder?' He answered, 'As you have said, I was a robber and a thief in the world, and because of this, taking me the Jews delivered me to the death of the cross together with our Lord Jesus Christ. While he still was upon the cross, seeing signs that happened I believed in him and called out to him and said, "Lord, when you reign as king, do not forget me." And immediately he said to me, "Truly, truly, today I say to you, you will be with me in paradise."[df] So I came, carrying my cross, into paradise, and found Michael the archangel, and said to him, "Our Lord Jesus Christ who was crucified has sent me here; so bring me to the gate of Eden." And when the flaming sword saw the sign of the cross, it opened for me and I entered in. Then the archangel said to me, "Wait a short time, for Adam

---

db. Or "forefathers"
dc. Psa 118:26 (LXX)
dd. Or "forefather"
de. Gen 5:24; Rev 11:3-12
df. Luke 23:43

the ancestor[dg] of humanity[dh] comes with the righteous, that they may also enter in. And now, having seen you, I come to greet you." ' And upon hearing these things, the saints shouted out with a loud voice, saying, 'Great is our Lord, and great is his power!' "

11.1 "We ourselves saw and heard all these things, *we* the two brothers, who also were sent by Michael the archangel and appointed to preach the resurrection of the Lord, but first to go to the Jordan and be baptized, where we also went and were baptized, together with other dead who had risen again. Then we also went to Jerusalem and completed the Passover of the resurrection. But now we depart, for we are not able to stay in this place. And the love of God and the Father, and the grace of our Lord Jesus Christ, and the fellowship of the Holy Spirit be with you all."

Upon writing these things and sealing the books, they gave half to the chief priests and half to Joseph and Nicodemus. And they themselves immediately vanished.

To the glory of our Lord Jesus Christ. Amen.

SELECT BIBLIOGRAPHY

Ehrman, Bart D., and Zlatko Pleše. *The Apocryphal Gospels: Texts and Translations*. Oxford: Oxford University Press, 2010.

James, M. R. *The Apocryphal New Testament*. Oxford: Clarendon, 1924.

Klauck, Hans-Josef. *Apocryphal Gospels: An Introduction*. London: T&T Clark, 2004.

Tischendorf, C. von. *Evangelia Apocrypha*. 2nd ed. Leipzig: Mendelssohn, 1876.

---

dg. Or "forefather"
dh. Or "mankind"

— The Gospel of Mary (Greek Portions)

INTRODUCTION

Like the *Gospel of Thomas*, the *Gospel of Mary* (*Gos. Mary*) has its largest extant portion in a Coptic manuscript.[a] It was discovered in a bound codex in the late 19th century and purchased by a German scholar, Carl Reinhardt, who deposited it in the Egyptian Museum in Berlin.[b] The codex contains not only *Gos. Mary* but also *The Apocryphon of John, Sophia of Jesus Christ*,[c] and a lesser-known work called *The Act of Peter*.[d] Although work on a critical edition began shortly after the codex was brought to Berlin, a series of unfortunate circumstances, not to mention two world wars, delayed publication until 1955.[e] The material extant in Coptic for *Gos. Mary* is incomplete, as the codex is missing pages 1–6 and 11–14.[f]

In 1938 the Rylands Library published a Greek manuscript containing part of *Gos. Mary*, P.Ryl. 463.[g] This single papyrus leaf, with clear writing on both sides, dates to the third century.[h]

---

a. The "Mary" of *Gos. Mary* is likely Mary Magdalene, not Mary the mother of Jesus.

b. Bart D. Ehrman and Zlatko Pleše, *The Apocryphal Gospels: Texts and Translations* (Oxford: Oxford University Press, 2010), 587.

c. Pheme Perkins, "Mary, Gospel of," *ABD* 4:583.

d. Ehrman and Pleše, *The Apocryphal Gospels*, 587. Perkins does not mention *The Act of Peter*, but Ehrman and Pleše do; they also specify that it is different from the more widely known *Acts of Peter*.

e. Ibid., 587–88.

f. Ibid., 588.

g. C. H. Roberts, "463. The Gospel of Mary," in *Catalogue of the Greek and Latin Papyri in the John Rylands Library* (Manchester: University of Manchester Press, 1938), 3:18–23.

h. Ehrman and Pleše, *The Apocryphal Gospels*, 588.

In 1983 another Greek fragment was published in volume 50 of the Oxyrhynchus Papyri.[i] This papyrus fragment, which also dates to the third century, is likely from a roll.[j] It uses a documentary hand, which means it may have been prepared by a non-professional scribe for private use.[k]

Both Greek fragments contain content that is also witnessed in the Coptic material.

Content

The *Gospel of Mary* has a framework that "draws on a motif found in a number of Christian gnostic writings ... where the risen Lord instructs the disciples in the secret gnostic teaching which they are to spread in the world."[l] As such, *Gos. Mary* differs from other apocryphal gospels included in this work in that its material includes only post-resurrection appearances of Jesus. Further, the material (particularly that extant only in Coptic) is much more overtly gnostic than other fragmentary materials included in this work.

P.Oxy. 3525 contains material similar to that found in chapters (pages) 9–10 of the Coptic *Gos. Mary*. It is a dialogue that takes place after the risen Jesus has gone away, and the disciples are distraught and afraid. Mary Magdalene then issues a stirring response to their fear, and "changed their mind." From here, the fragment trails off with Mary recalling the teaching of Jesus, instructing the disciples in things hidden to them, but known to Mary.

P.Ryl. 463 contains material similar to that found in chapters (pages) 17–19 of the Coptic *Gos. Mary*, which end the gospel. This is apparently the end of Mary's discourse on the hidden things. After Mary's conclusion, Andrew disputes Mary's contention that she is repeating the teaching of Jesus because it is unfamiliar to him. Peter seems similarly hesitant, wondering why Jesus would tell these secret things to a woman instead of speaking them openly. After this, Levi rebukes Peter as always being angry,

---

i. P. J. Parsons, "3525. Gospel of Mary" (London: Egypt Exploration Society, 1983), 12–14.

j. Macquarie University, "Gospel of Mary," *XVI Excerpts from Apocryphal Books*, 2005, http://mq.edu.au/pubstatic/public/download/?id=45136; Ehrman and Pleše, *The Apocryphal Gospels*, 588.

k. Macquarie University, "Gospel of Mary."

l. Perkins, "Mary, Gospel of," 4:583.

and urges the group to do "that which has been commanded to us," which he equates with preaching the gospel. He then leaves[m] to begin to preach the gospel; at which point *Gos. Mary* ends.

TRANSLATION

Transcription and reconstruction of P.Oxy. 3525 is based on official images from the Oxyrhynchus Papyri Online[n] in consultation with Ehrman and Pleše[o] and the transcription found in Macquarie University's *Papyri from the Rise of Christianity in Egypt*.[p]

Transcription and reconstruction of P.Ryl. 463 are based on official images from the John Rylands Library[q] in consultation with Ehrman and Pleše.[r] Transcription and translation follow Ehrman and Pleše's labeling of recto and verso;[s] these appear to differ with photographs of the papyri available from the Rylands Library.

P.Oxy. 3525

Reading Translation

FRAGMENT 1: Recto. ... nothing ... Upon saying these things, he went out. And they grieved, weeping greatly and saying, "How can we go to the nations preaching the gospel of the kingdom of the Son of Man? For if they did not spare that one, how will they spare us?" Then Mary arose and, greeting them, she kissed everyone and said, "Brothers, do not weep or grieve or doubt, for the grace of him will be with you, watching over you. Instead let us give thanks to his greatness, because he has knit us together and made us people." Upon saying these things, Mary changed

---

m. In the Coptic, "they" leave (meaning the whole group, the disciples and Mary Magdalene) instead of just Levi.

n. "P.Oxy.L 3525," *POxy: Oxyrhynchus Online*, http://www.papyrology.ox.ac.uk/POxy/

o. Ehrman and Pleše, *The Apocryphal Gospels*, 600–601.

p. Macquarie University, "Gospel of Mary."

q. John Rylands University Library, "Gospel of Mary - Rylands Papri - Greek Papyrus 463 - Recto," *John Rylands University Library Image Collections*, n.d.; John Rylands University Library, "Gospel of Mary - Rylands Papri - Greek Papyrus 463 - Verso," *John Rylands University Library Image Collections*, n.d.

r. Ehrman and Pleše, *The Apocryphal Gospels*, 602–605.

s. Ibid.

their mind to good and they began to debate concerning the sayings of the Savior. Peter said to Mary, "Sister, we know that you were greatly loved by the Savior as no other woman. Tell us, therefore, whatever you know of the words of the Savior which we have not heard." Mary replied, saying, "Whatever escapes your notice and I remember, I will tell you." And she began with these words to them: "Once in a vision, I, seeing the Lord, I said, 'Lord, today …' "

Verso. [blank]

Line Translation

FRAGMENT 1: Recto

1
2
3   [...] nothing … [...]
4   …
5   [t]hese things Upon saying, he we[nt out. And they grieved]
6   [weeping greatly and] saying, "How can we [go to the nations]
7   [preaching the gos]pel of the kin[gdom of the Son of Man? If]
8   [for not that one they did sp]are, how us will [they spare?" Then arose Mar-]
9   [y and greeting] them she kissed [everyone and said, "Brothers,]
10 [not do weep or gr]ieve or doubt, the [for grace of him will be]
11 [w]ith you watching over you. Instead let us give th[anks to the greatne-]
12 [s]s of him, because he has knit together us and peopl[e made us." Upon saying these things,]
13 [Mar]y turned over the mind of them t[o good and they began to]

14 [d]eb[at]e concerning the sayings of the Savi[or. Peter said

15 [t]o Mary, "Sister, we know that great[ly you were loved by the]

16 [Sav]ior as no other woman. Tell, therefore, to us what[ever you know of]

17 [the wor]ds of the Savior which we not have heard." Rep[lied Mary, say-]

18 [ing, "Whatever] escapes your notice and I remember, I will te[ll you." And she began to]

19 [them the]se wor[ds:] "I once in a vision, se[eing the Lord,]

20 [I said,] 'Lord, today [——]

Verso. [blank]

P.RYL. 463

Reading Translation

FRAGMENT 1: Recto. 21 ... the remaining course of the time of time of the age, rest in silence. Having said these things, Mary was silent as if it was the Savior who had been speaking until now. Andrew said, "Brothers, what do you think about the ... of what has been said? For indeed, I myself do not believe these things the Savior has said, for it seems to be different than the thinking of that one. Upon questioning about these matters, did the Savior secretly speak to a woman, and plainly, that we all might hear? Did he want to show that she is even more important than us?" ...

Verso. 22 ... of the Savior?" Levi said to Peter, "Peter, anger always lies beside you, and so now you are debating with the woman as if you are her enemy. If the Savior considered her worthy, who are you to disdain her? For that one, always knowing her, surely loved her. Instead, let us be ashamed and, being clothed with the perfect human, that which has been commanded to us, let us do. Let us preach the gospel, no longer being angry or making laws, as the Savior said." Upon saying these things, Levi indeeed went away, beginning to preach ...

Line Translation

FRAGMENT 1: Recto

1   21
2   the remaining course of the t[im]e of time
3   of the age, rest i[n] silence. These
4   thin[gs] having said, Mary was sil-
5   en[t] as if the Savior until now
6   had been speaking. Andrew said, "Broth-
7   ers, what do you thin[k] abo[u]t the..
8   .. of what has been said? [I indeed]
9   for not I do believe these things the Sa-
10 vior has said, it seems f[or to be]
11 different than the of that one mi-]
12 nd. Concerning the[s]e ma[tt-]
13 ers, upon questioning the Sav[ior]
14 secretly to a woman did speak, and pl[ai-]
15 nly, that all we might h[ear?]
16 [not ev]en more importa[nt than us her]
17 [to show did h]e[want?]

Verso

1   22
2   ... of the Savior?" Lev[i] said to Pet[er,]
3   "Peter, alw[ays] to yo[u] anger lies bes-
4   ide and so now you are debatin[g] with the
5   woman [a]s if being set against her.
6   If the Savior considered her worthy,
7   who are you to disdain her? Alwa-
8   y[s] for that one, knowing her [su-]
9   r[e]l[y] loved her. Inste[a]d le[t] us be
10 a[sham]ed and, being clothed wi[th] the
11 p[erfec]t human, that which ha[s] been

12 co[mmanded to] us, let us do. Let us pre-
13 a[ch the] gos[p]el, no longer bei[ng] ang-
14 r[y o]r making laws, as sa-
15 i[d the] Savior. Upon sa[y]ing [the]se things, Le[v]-
16 [i inde]eed went [away] beginning to p[rea-]
17 [ch ...]

SELECT BIBLIOGRAPHY

Ehrman, Bart D., and Zlatko Pleše. *The Apocryphal Gospels: Texts and Translations*. Oxford: Oxford University Press, 2010.

John Rylands University Library. "Gospel of Mary - Rylands Papri - Greek Papyrus 463 - Recto." *John Rylands University Library Image Collections*, n.d. Available online.

———. "Gospel of Mary - Rylands Papri - Greek Papyrus 463 - Verso." *John Rylands University Library Image Collections*, n.d. Available online.

Macquarie University. "Gospel of Mary." *XVI Excerpts from Apocryphal Books*, 2005. http://mq.edu.au/pubstatic/public/download/?id=45136.

"P.Oxy.L 3525." *POxy: Oxyrhynchus Online*. http://www.papyrology.ox.ac.uk/POxy/

Parsons, P. J. "3525. Gospel of Mary." Pages 12–14 in vol. 50 of *The Oxyrhynchus Papyri*. London: Egypt Exploration Society, 1983.

Perkins, Pheme. "Mary, Gospel of." *ABD* 4:583–84.

Roberts, C. H. "463. The Gospel of Mary." Pages 18–23 in vol. 3 of *Catalogue of the Greek and Latin Papyri in the John Rylands Library*. Manchester: University of Manchester Press, 1938.

— *Fragments*

"Fragments" refer to ancient pieces of papyrus and parchment. Thousands of fragments and even complete works have been found in places such as Oxyrhynchus, ranging from tax receipts to classical works of literature to personal letters. Some of these fragments witness the earliest known forms of canonical material. And some of them witness stories of Jesus that were long forgotten, helping provide a fuller understanding of Christianity in the first few centuries after the time of Christ.

VOCABULARY

The study of these manuscript fragments, known as papyrology, has its own specialized vocabulary. Here is some basic terminology:

- **Papyrus:** A paper-like writing surface developed in ancient Egypt. It was created from the reeds of the papyrus plant, which were stripped of bark and sliced into thin strips. The strips were placed in two layers, at right angles to each other, then pounded and smoothed.[a]

- **Parchment:** A writing surface made from animal skins, typically those of sheep or goats. The hair is removed, then the skin is stretched, treated, and dried. After drying, it is rubbed smooth with pumice and then finally dressed with chalk. It provided a higher quality surface than papyrus, but was also more expensive.[b]

---

a. E. J. Goodspeed and I. A. Sparks, "Papyrus," *ISBE* 3:651.
b. I. A. Sparks, "Parchment," *ISBE* 3:663.

- **Recto:** The surface of papyrus that has the fibers of the papyrus plant layered horizontally. It is typically the easiest surface of the papyrus to write upon, and is usually found to be the first side written upon (in a page or codex) or the only side written upon (in a papyrus roll).

- **Verso:** The surface of papyrus that has the fibers of the papyrus plant layered vertically. It is typically the more difficult surface of the papyrus to write upon.

SOURCES

Fragments of papyrus and parchment are usually published in larger collections. The most well-known collection is the Oxyrhynchus Papyri, gathered from a series of digs in Oxyrhynchus, Egypt, in the early 20th century. To date, more than 5,000 papyri and parchments have been published in more than 75 volumes by the Egypt Exploration Society, and many more remain to be published. There are also private and museum collections that contain fragmentary witnesses to noncanonical gospels.

The collection of Greek fragments in this book are as follows:[c]

- Dura Parchment 24

- P.Berol. 11710

- P.Cairo 10735

- P.Egerton 2 (with P.Köln 255)

- P.Merton 51

- P.Oxy. 210

- P.Oxy. 840

---

c. Andrew Bernhard, *Other Early Christian Gospels: A Critical Edition of the Surviving Greek Manuscripts* (T&T Clark International, 2007); Bart D. Ehrman and Zlatko Pleše, *The Apocryphal Gospels: Texts and Translations* (Oxford: Oxford University Press, 2010); M. R. James, *The Apocryphal New Testament* (Oxford: Clarendon, 1924); Wilhelm Schneemelcher, ed., *New Testament Apocrypha*, rev. ed., trans. R. McL. Wilson, (Louisville: Westminster John Knox, 1991). These references were consulted in determining the makeup this collection of fragmentary gospel material. Unless otherwise noted, transcriptions and translations are the author's.

- P.Oxy. 1224

- P.Oxy. 5072

- P.Vindobonensis G. 2325

Each of these fragments will be introduced with some discussion as to its relevance to biblical studies.

USE OF FRAGMENTS IN BIBLICAL STUDIES

Fragmentary witnesses to otherwise unknown gospels provide examples of different ways in which early generations of Christians interacted with canonical material. They contain stories of Jesus (authentic or not) that would otherwise be unknown, and they can even provide linguistic insight through infrequent vocabulary and syntactic structures.

One important step when considering the text of a fragment of an unknown gospel is to consider possible canonical parallels. Is similar language used in the New Testament or the Septuagint? Are similar things discussed in other noncanonical material?

Another step when considering a fragment is to realize what material is witnessed by the fragment and what material is supplied. Transcriptions of fragments typically include reconstructed material, denoted by [brackets]. The reconstructed material is supplied by the editor of a transcription. It is the best guess of the editor as to what material can be reliably restored in order to make sense of the fragment. Firm conclusions or assertions should not be made by appeal to something found only in reconstructed text.[d] An example would be the use of Φαρισαιοι (Pharisaioi, "Pharisees") in P.Merton 51, which the original editors date in the third century.[e] The use of "Pharisee" attested outside of the New Testament in this time frame, in the context of the papyrus (here a discussion of baptism), could be important.

d. Thomas J. Kraus, "Reconstructing Fragmentary Manuscripts—Chances and Limitations," in *Early Christian Manuscripts*, ed. T. J. Kraus and T. Nicklas, Texts and Editions for New Testament Study 5 (Leiden: Brill, 2010), 1–3.

e. B. R. Rees, "51. Christian Fragment," in *A Descriptive Catalogue of the Greek Papyri in the Collection of Wilfred Merton, F.S.A.*, ed. B. R. Rees, Sir Harold I. Bell, and J. W. B. Barns, Merton Papyri (Dublin: Hodges Figgis, 1959), 2:1.

However, because it occurs only in reconstructed text it is best to not use P.Merton 51 as primary evidence in a discussion about Pharisees.

Lastly, ask whether the fragment provides information previously unknown about Jesus or any other topic, and how that material correlates with what is already known. Another example involving a Pharisee is from P.Oxy. 840, which refers to someone who is both a chief priest and a Pharisee. Is this combination attested elsewhere, or is it unknown? Is it even possible? Working through these sorts of questions involves stepping into the world of the fragment as much as possible and comparing it to the world of what is actually known. This helps establish how the writer and readers of the unknown gospel material used it. This, in turn, can help modern readers understand aspects of the fragmentary material and how it relates to the understanding of Jesus.

DURA PARCHMENT 24

DESCRIPTION

The ancient city of Dura was destroyed in AD 256–257.[f] Dura Parchment 24 is a small parchment (9.5 × 10.5cm) that was discovered in an embankment in the ruins of the city.[g] Kraeling reports, "Judging from its condition and outward appearance when found, it had been crushed in the hand and thrown away as a piece of waste paper."[h] As waste, it became part of an embankment intended to protect the city from a Roman siege. Because the date of the siege is relatively secure, this fragment is usually dated to the first half of the third century.[i] The paleographical details of the parchment support this dating.[j]

The original evaluation of the parchment concluded it to be a fragment of Tatian's *Diatessaron*, an early gospel harmony.[k] Scholars today agree on

---

f. Ehrman and Pleše, *The Apocryphal Gospels*, 232.

g. Carl H. Kraeling, *A Greek Fragment of Tatian's Diatessaron from Dura: Edited with Facsimile, Transcription, and Introduction*, Studies and Documents 3 (London: Christophers, 1935), 3.

h. Ibid.

i. Ibid., 5–7. Kraeling suggests the year 222.

j. Ibid., 4–5.

k. Kraeling, *A Greek Fragment of Tatian's Diatessaron from Dura*.

the parchment's status as a gospel harmony, although some are not convinced that it is a fragment of the *Diatessaron.*[1]

Content Highlights

As it is likely a gospel harmony, the parchment has a tight relationship with the text of the canonical Gospels. It represents material found in Matt 27:56–57; Mark 15:40–42; Luke 23:49–51; and John 19:38. The parchment begins with the women who followed Jesus, including Salome and probably the mother of the sons of Zebedee, going to see the body of Jesus. It records that it was the "evening of preparation," the day before the Sabbath. It describes Joseph of Arimathea as a "disciple of Jesus" who was "anticipating the kingdom of God" as well as recording his disagreement with the council (Sanhedrin).

Relevance for Exegesis

Dura Parchment 24, in its first two lines, refers to "the wives of those who had followed him from Galilee" as part of the group, along with Salome and (probably) the mother of the sons of Zebedee, who all went to see "the crucified one." This rests on reconstructed text, and is different from what is found in the canonical Gospels, which refer either to specifically named women or a generic group of women who had been following Jesus. The difference lies in reading lines 1–2 as αι γυναικες [των συ]νακολουθησαντων ("the wives [of those who] had followed") or as [εκ τω]ν ακολουθησαντων ("the women [from among those who] had followed"). Kraeling supports the first option,[m] although Parker, Taylor and Goodacre convincingly argue for the second option,[n] which also seems to better align with the canonical form of the text.

---

1. D. C. Parker, D. K. G. Taylor, and M. S. Goodacre, "The Dura-Europos Gospel Harmony," in *Studies in the Early Text of the Gospels and Acts: The Papers of the First Birmingham Colloquium on the Textual Criticism of the New Testament*, ed. D. K. G. Taylor, Text-Critical Studies (Atlanta: Society of Biblical Literature, 1999), 192–228.

m. Kraeling, *A Greek Fragment*, 28–30.

n. Parker, Taylor, and Goodacre, "Studies in the Early Text of the Gospels and Acts."

Dura Parchment 24 also gives a concise picture of Joseph of Arimathea, merging the assertion in the Gospel of John that he was a "secret disciple" (John 19:38) with Luke's description (Luke 23:50).

TRANSLATION

Reading Translation

FRAGMENT 1: Recto. ... Zebedee and Salome and the wives of those who had followed him from Galilee to see the crucified one. And it was the day of preparation; the Sabbath was beginning. And when it was evening of the preparation, that is the before Sabbath, there came a man of the council, being from Arimathea, a city of Judea, the name of Joseph, a good, righteous person, being a disciple of Jesus, but secretly because of the fear of the Jews. And he was anticipating the kingdom of God. This person not was in agreement with the council ...

Line Translation

FRAGMENT 1: Recto

1   [Zebed]ee and Salome a[n]d the wives
2   [of those who] had followed h[i]m from
3   [Galil]ee to see the crucified one. And it was
4   [the da]y of preparation; the Sabbath was begin-
5   [ning.] And when it was evening of the prep-
6   [aration], that is the before Sabbath, there
7   [came] a man of the council, [b]e-
8   ing from Arimathe[a], a city of
9   [Jude]a, the name of Joseph, a good, ri
10 [ghteous person], being a disciple of Jesus, se-
11 [cret]ly But because of the fear of the
12 [Jew]s. And he was anticipating
13 [the] k[ingdom] of God. This person not
14 [was in agree]ment with the cou[ncil]

P.BEROL. 11710

Description

P.Berol. 11710 is a miniature codex[o] consisting of two small leaves. It is bilingual, as the content of fragment B recto is Coptic ("Jesus Christ God"). The papyrus was first published in 1923[p] and is usually dated to the sixth century.[q]

Content Highlights

P.Berol. 11710 contains an exchange between Jesus and Nathanael. It is notable for including the phrase "Rabbi Lord" as well as Nathanael's testimony that Jesus is the Son of God. It has strong parallels with the Gospel of John (John 1:29, 49), repeating John the Baptist's testimony about the lamb of God (John 1:29), but from the lips of Nathanael. Further, the papyrus seems to interact with Nathanael being "under a fig tree" (John 1:50, when Philip initially told Nathanael about Jesus), with Jesus instructing him to "walk in the sun,"[r] perhaps also referring to the common darkness/light motif found in the Gospel of John.

The Coptic text and abbreviations found on the fourth page of the miniature codex have been much neglected. Kraus gives the fullest treatment.[s] In his estimation, outside of the nomina sacra representing "Jesus Christ," the meaning of the abbreviations and ligatures are uncertain, though they may point to a co-equal relationship between the Father and the Son.

Relevance for Exegesis

The primary importance of P.Berol. 11710 in the context of canonical material is the relationship it seems to have with the Gospel of John. The calling of Philip and Nathanael (John 1:43–51) contains Nathanael's testimony of

---

o. H. Lietzmann, "Ein apokryphes Evangelienfragment," *ZNW* 22 (1923): 153–54; Thomas J. Kraus, "2. P.Berol 11710," in *Gospel Fragments*, ed. Thomas J. Kraus, Michael J. Kruger, and Tobias Nicklas, Oxford Early Christian Gospel Texts (Oxford: Oxford University Press, 2009), 228–29. Lietzmann considers the papyrus to be an amulet, not a miniature codex. Kraus (237) helpfully argues that the papyrus was likely created as a miniature codex, but could have subsequently been used as an amulet.

p. Lietzmann, "Ein apokryphes Evangelienfragment."

q. Kraus, "2. P.Berol 11710," 229; Bernhard, *Other Early Christian Gospels*, 102.

r. Kraus, "2. P.Berol 11710," 233.

s. Ibid., 235–237.

Jesus, "Rabbi, you are the Son of God!" (John 1:49). This similarity with the first four lines of the papyrus ties the noncanonical exchange in P.Berol. 11710 with the first chapter of John.

Further, the author of P.Berol. 11710 has put the words of John the Baptist's testimony, "The Lamb of God who takes away the sin of the world" (John 1:29), into the mouth of Nathanael, only directly spoken to Jesus: "Rabbi Lord, you are the lamb of God who takes away the sins of the world."

The final point of contact with the Gospel of John is more subtle. In P.Berol. 11710, Jesus urges Nathanael to "walk in the sun." The word translated "walk" is πορευου, a middle/passive imperative. Jesus' response to Nathanael's testimony is an exhortation to "walk in the sun." It is possible that this statement refers to the light/dark motif found in Johannine literature, particularly the notion that "walking in the light" is akin to following Jesus (John 8:12; 11:9, 10; 12:35; 1 John 1:7).

This papyrus witnesses a Christianity where Jesus is called "Rabbi" (as he is several times in John; see 1:38, 49; 3:2; 4:31; 6:25; 9:2; 11:8), but also "Rabbi Lord," which is not testified in the New Testament. The papyrus witnesses Jesus called the Son of God and also the lamb of God who takes away the sin of the world as well as, possibly a light/dark motif similar to that used by John's Gospel.

TRANSLATION

Reading Translation

FRAGMENT A: Verso. ... and he said, "Rabbi Lord, you are the Son of God." The Rabbi also said, "Nathanael,

Recto. walk in the sun." Nathanael answered him and said, "Rabbi Lord, you are the lamb

FRAGMENT B: Verso. of God who takes away the sins of the world." The Rabbi answered him and said, ...

Recto. Jesus Christ God

Line Translation

Fragment A: Verso

    1   ... and
    2   he said, "Rabb-
    3   i Lord, you are the So-
    4   n of God."
    5   The Rabbi also
    6   said, "Natha-
    7   nael,

Recto

    1   walk in th-
    2   e sun." Answe-
    3   red him Na-
    4   thanael and
    5   said, "Rab-
    6   bi Lord, you are
    7   the lamb

Fragment B: Verso

    1   of God who takes
    2   away the si-
    3   ns of the wor-
    4   ld." Answe-
    5   red him the R-
    6   abbi and
    7   said, ...

Recto

    1   Jesus Christ Go-
    2   d

P.CAIRO 10735

DESCRIPTION

P.Cairo 10735 is a single leaf of papyrus with writing on both sides. Grenfell and Hunt note it is "out of a book containing apparently an uncanonical gospel."[t] There is some dispute as to whether it is in the gospel genre. Deissmann argues that it "contains some kind of *reflections* on the flight into Egypt and the words of Gabriel, reflections either of an exegetical or edifying nature, and that instead of coming from a gospel it comes from a commentary or a book of sermons."[u] Grenfell and Hunt date the papyrus to the sixth or seventh century.[v]

The transcription[w] and translation are presented in the traditional order (recto, verso). However, it is possible the original order is verso, recto, as this would provide a chronological order to the material.[x]

CONTENT HIGHLIGHTS

This papyrus witnesses two distinct episodes. Both episodes involve angelic witness and testimony regarding the birth and childhood of Jesus.

The episode on the recto opens with the angel of the Lord imploring Joseph to take his wife and flee into Egypt. The language immediately brings to mind Matt 2:13, which records much of this same material. However, the material that follows in the papyrus (mentioning "every gift" and "his friends" and a king) cannot be reconciled with Matthew, and remains a mystery.[y]

The verso material includes an episode reminiscent of Luke 1:36, the angelic announcement to Mary that her relative, Elizabeth, is pregnant.

---

t. Bernard P. Grenfell and Arthur S. Hunt, eds., *Catalogue Général des Antiquitiés Égyptiennes du Musée du Caire, Nos. 10001–10869: Greek Papyri* (Oxford: University Press, 1903), 90.

u. Adolf Deissmann, *Light from the Ancient East: The New Testament Illustrated by Recently Discovered Texts of the Graeco-Roman World*, trans. Lionel Richard Mortimer Strachan (London: Hodder & Stoughton, 1910), 442. Italics are Deissmann's.

v. Grenfell and Hunt, *Greek Papyri*, 90.

w. Deissmann, *Light from the Ancient East*, 441; Thomas J. Kraus, "3. P.Cair.G 10735," in *Gospel Fragments*, 248. Photographs of P.Cair. 10735 are not available; the transcription is therefore that of Deissmann, checked against that of Kraus.

x. Kraus, "3. P.Cair.G 10735," 248.

y. Ibid.

The significance of Elizabeth's pregnancy (and the announcement of it) is briefly discussed.

RELEVANCE FOR EXEGESIS

Whether a gospel, a commentary, or a sermon, P.Cairo 10735 is important for recording alternate versions of material also known in the canonical infancy narratives.

The material on the recto, although similar to Matt 2:13, is different from the canonical material in that Joseph is instructed to flee with Mary; there is no mention of the child Jesus. In Matthew, Jesus is the center of attention ("take the child and his mother"), but in P.Cairo 10735, it is only Mary ("take Mary your wife").[z]

The material on the recto (lines 2–5) uses the words of Luke 1:36, but in somewhat different order. In this episode Mary is the primary figure. Line 1 refers to "you," which in context must be Mary, but this is only known by material in line 2, which refers to "the virgin" (παρθενος, *parthenos*) as the one being spoken to.[aa] After the material witnessed in Luke, a summary and explanation occurs. The announcement of John is explained as a necessary precursor to the announcement to Mary of the coming of Jesus. While the theme of John necessarily preceding Jesus is found in the New Testament, a succinct and unambiguous statement of its necessity—and the necessity of the "commander of the host of angels" to make this announcement—is not found in canonical material.

TRANSLATION

Reading Translation

FRAGMENT 1: Recto. The angel of the Lord said, "Joseph, get up, take Mary your wife and flee into Egypt and ... every gift and if ... his friends ... of the king ..."

---

z. It should be noted, however, that portions of this material are reconstructed and that the reconstructions, while sensible, may be incorrect.

aa. The simple reference to Mary as "the virgin" argues for a later date to the material witnessed in this papyrus.

Verso. ... let it be explained to you. Now the commander of the host of angels said to the virgin, "Behold, Elizabeth, your relative, even she has conceived and is in her sixth month, the one called barren." In the sixth month, which is Thoth, John's mother conceived. And it was imperative that the commander of the host of angels proclaim John in advance, the house-servant going before the appearance of his Lord....

Line Translation

FRAGMENT 1: Recto

1 The angel of the Lord said, "Jo[seph, get up,]
2 take Mary the w[ife of you and]
3 flee into Egypt and
4 [...]
5 [...]
6 every gift and if
7 his friends
8 of the king
9 [...]
10 [...]"

Verso

1 ... let it be explained to you. the [Now]
2 [commander of the host of angels] said to the virgin, "Behold,
3 [Elizabeth, the rel]ative of you, even she has
4 [conceived and six]th is in her month, the one ca[ll-]
5 [ed barren." In] the sixth, which is [Thoth, mon-]
6 [th, the mother of Jo]hn conceived.
7 [And it was imperative to procl]aim the commander of the host
8 [of angels John, th]e house-servant going bef-
9 [ore the of his Lord] appearance.
10 [...]
11 [...]

P.EGERTON 2 (WITH P.KÖLN 255)[A][B]

DESCRIPTION

The publication of P.Egerton 2 in 1935 grabbed the attention of the New Testament studies world. It is an ancient Christian papyrus fragment, initially dated to the "middle of the second century."[ac] This made it the earliest known Christian fragment of any sort, even earlier than the canonical material then available. It had the interest of many—Ehrman notes "some fifty scholarly articles devoted to it within three years."[ad] However, the furor died down with the publication of P.Ryl. 457 (P52), which has a stronger claim on being the earliest Christian manuscript,[ae] typically dated in the range of AD 100–150.[af]

However, the story was not over. More than 50 years later, in 1987, Gronewald located a small fragment known as P.Köln 255, which he asserted was actually a portion of fragment 1 of P.Egerton 2.[ag] His judgment has been confirmed, and now editions of P.Egerton 2 include P.Köln 255 as a portion of fragment 1, placed at the recto bottom left corner / verso bottom right corner.

The advent of P.Köln 255 allowed for more evidence to review the initial dating of the manuscript. Gronewald suggested a date of AD 200; Nicklas suggests "towards the end of the second or even in the first decades of the third century CE."[ah]

CONTENT HIGHLIGHTS

P.Egerton 2 (with P.Köln 255) is one of the larger fragmentary witnesses of a noncanonical gospel available. Two fragments, each with more than 20

---

ab. Translation is only given for the first two fragments; the third and fourth fragments do not contain enough text to reliably translate. The order fragment 1 verso, recto; fragment 2 recto, verso is the order followed by most editions.

ac. Sir Harold I. Bell and T.C. Skeat, eds., *Fragments of an Unknown Gospel and Other Early Christian Papyri*, New impression (London: British Museum Press, 1935), 1.

ad. Ehrman and Pleše, *The Apocryphal Gospels*, 246.

ae. Tobias Nicklas, "I. The 'Unknown Gospel' on Papyrus Egerton 2 (+ Papyrus Cologne 255)," in *Gospel Fragments*, 12.

af. Ehrman and Pleše, *The Apocryphal Gospels*, 245–46.

ag. Michael Gronewald, "255. Unbekanntes Evangelium oder Evangelienharmonie (Fragment aus dem Evangelium Egerton)," in *Kölner Papyri*, ed. Michael Gronewald, et al. (Opladen: Westdeutscher Verlag, 1987), 6:136; Nicklas, "I. The 'Unknown Gospel'," 13.

ah. Nicklas, "I. The 'Unknown Gospel'," 21.

lines of writing on both sides, allude to or borrow from known canonical content without reproducing it exactly. At least one story is completely unknown elsewhere.

There are four primary episodes. First is an account of Jesus interacting with some who oppose Him, exhorting them to "search the scriptures" and warning them that "Moses" (thus, the Old Testament Law) accuses them. The crowd, reacting to Jesus' exhortation and accusation, attempts to arrest and stone Him. From here, after noting "his hour of handing over had not yet come," Jesus "went out through their midst and departed from them."

Next is an account of Jesus healing a leper. The leper explains that he became leprous while traveling and eating with lepers. He then tells Jesus, "If, then, you are willing, I will be made clean." Jesus heals him and instructs him to show himself to the priests and to "offer for your purification as Moses commanded, and sin no longer."

This is followed by an account of Jesus being questioned "pointedly" by people who ask the question, "is it right to give to kings what belongs to their rule? Shall we pay them or not?" Jesus does not give a direct answer, but instead accuses them of wanting to have their own preferences validated instead of truly learning from the teacher. Jesus explicitly references Isa 29:13 in his answer.

The first three accounts are at least familiar with similar synoptic accounts, either retelling them in different language or inventing similar accounts based on synoptic language. The last episode has no direct canonical parallel.[ai] It involves Jesus walking along the bank of the Jordan and, apparently, sowing seed. The final lines imply there was some miraculous growth, and the seed brought forth fruit. Ehrman notes this could be "possibly to illustrate [Jesus'] parable about the miraculous growth of seeds."[aj]

RELEVANCE FOR EXEGESIS

Three of the four episodes in the two primary fragments of P.Egerton 2 (+ P.Köln 255) reflect content found in the Synoptic Gospels.[ak] The first episode, where Jesus interacts with lawyers who oppose him, has Johannine

---

ai. Ibid., 74–75.

aj. Ehrman and Pleše, *The Apocryphal Gospels*, 245.

ak. Bell and Skeat, *Fragments of an Unknown Gospel*; Ehrman and Pleše, *The Apocryphal Gospels*, 248–53. Cross references in this section are largely derived from these two sources.

undertones. Lines 7–10 reflect John 5:39. Mention of Moses accusing those whom Jesus is addressing, from John 5:45, is found in lines 10–14. The reply of the opponents in lines 14–17, that Moses' origin is known, comes from John 9:29. And the reply of Jesus in lines 17–23 is, again, from John 5:46. Material from John's Gospel must have been available to the author, and he used it in crafting this account of Jesus and the lawyers.

This episode likely continues onto the other side of fragment 1, with the crowd looking to stone Jesus (lines 1–8); this has similarities with John 7:30; 7:44; 8:59 and 10:31. Lines 9–10 mention "the Lord himself" escaping from the crowd, this has parallels with John 10:39 and Luke 4:30.

The second episode is a story of Jesus, referred to as "teacher Jesus," healing a leper (lines 9–23). Similar episodes are found in the Synoptic Gospels, in Matt 8:2–4; Mark 1:40–44; and Luke 5:12–16. The account here shares some elements with the synoptic accounts, including the Lord's response of "I am willing; be made clean." Some of the post-cleansing instructions, such as going to the priests and offering the purification prescribed by the law of Moses, are also shared. However, the leper's explanation of how he contracted leprosy is not present in the synoptic accounts, and is valuable addition. The leper explains that he likely contracted leprosy when he was ministering to lepers. This may, in the mind of the author, provide some justification for the mercy that the Lord has upon the leper.

The third episode, on fragment 2, which also refers to Jesus as "teacher Jesus," begins in the midst of some intense questioning of Jesus, likely by his opponents (compare John 3:2; 10:25). The question is about "kings and their rule" and is reminiscent of the Synoptics' account of Jesus being questioned about paying taxes to Caesar (Matt 22:15–22; Mark 12:13–17; Luke 20:20–26). Jesus' answer, incomplete in the fragment, begins with a quotation of Isa 29:13, much like the parallel in Matt 15:7–9; Mark 7:6–7 does. The fragment breaks off in the middle of the quotation, so the complete response of Jesus is not known.

The fourth episode, taking place on the bank of the Jordan River, has no explicit ties to material found in the canonical Gospels.

TRANSLATION

Reading Translation

FRAGMENT 1: Verso. ... to the lawyers ... every wrongdoer ... and not me....
How he does what he does ... and turning to the rulers of the people, he
said this word, "Search the scriptures; in which you think to have life; these
are they who bear witness to me. Do not think that I came to accuse you
to my Father. There is one who accuses you, Moses, in whom you hope."
And they were saying, "We know well that Moses spoke to God, but you
we do not know where you are." Answering, Jesus said to them, "Now your
unbelief is accused by what he testified against. For if you believed Moses,
you would have believed me. For that one has written to your forefathers
concerning me."

Recto. ... the crowd ... stones together to stone him. And the rulers laid
their hands on him so that they might seize and hand him over to the
crowd. And they were not able to arrest him because his hour of being
handed over had not yet come. But the Lord himself went out through
their midst and departed from them. And behold, a leper, having come to
him, said: "Teacher Jesus, while traveling with lepers and eating with them
at the inn, I became a leper, even I myself. If, then, you are willing, I will
be made clean." Then the Lord said to him, "I am willing, be made clean."
And immediately the leprosy departed from him. And the Lord said to him,
"Go, show yourself to the priests and offer for your purification as Moses
commanded, and sin no longer."

FRAGMENT 2: Recto. ... coming to him, questioning him pointedly, saying,
"Teacher Jesus, we know that you have come from God. For the things you
do testify beyond all the prophets. Therefore you tell us: Is it right to give
to the kings what belongs to their rule? Shall we pay them or not?" And
Jesus, knowing their mind, indignantly said to them, "Why do you call me
with your mouth, 'Teacher,' not hearing what I say? Isaiah prophesied well

about you, saying, "This people honor me with their lips, but their heart is far away from me. Vainly they worship me ... commandments ..."

Verso. ... in place shut away ... placed underneath invisibly ... the weight of it unweighed ... And those, being confused as to his strange question. While walking, Jesus stood upon the bank of the Jordan river, and stretching his right hand, ... and he sowed it upon the ... and then ... water.... And before them and it brought forth fruit ... many ... for joy ...

Line Translation

Fragment 1: Verso

  1 [—]
  2 [.......]to the lawyers
  3 [... ev]ery wrongdo[er]
  4 [.....] and not me. [.].
  5 [.....]. how he does what he does
  6 [and the] rulers of the people turn-
  7 [ing to he]‖ said this word, sear-
  8 [ch t]he scriptures; in which you thi-
  9 [nk] life to have; these are they
10 [who bear] witness to me: not d[o]
11 [think th]at I came to accuse
12 [you] to the father of me. There is
13 [one who acc]uses you, Moses, in whom
14 [you] hope. And they were say-
15 [in]g, "We know well that to Moses spo-
16 [ke] God[,] but you we do not know
17 [where you are]. Answering, Jesus sa-
18 [id to the]m, "Now is accused
19 [your un]belie[f] by what he
20 [testfi]ed against. For if you be-
21 [lieved Moses,] you have believed wo[uld]
22 [me. conce]r[ning] For me that on[e]
23 [has writte]n to the fore[fa]thers of yo[u]

Recto

1 [... the cr]owd [.....—]
2 [......] stones together to [sto-]
3 n[e h]im. And they laid [the]
4 han[ds] of them on him the [rul-]
5 ers [so] that they might seize and hand [him]
6 o[ver] to the crowd. And not they [were able]
7 him to arrest because there not yet had come
8 his hour of handing [over]
9 But the Lord himself went out [through the midst th-]
10 eir departed from [them].
11 And behold, a leper, having com[e to him,]
12 said: "Teacher Jesus, le[pers with]
13 traveling and eatin[g with them]
14 at the inn, I became a l[eper],
15 even I myself. If, then, [you are willing,]
16 I will be made clean." Then the Lord [said to him,]
17 "I am willing, be made clean." [And immediately]
18 departed from him the lep[rosy. said]
19 And to him Jesus, "Go[, your-]
20 self show to th[e priests]
21 and offer [for your pur-]
22 [if]ication as com[m]a[nded Moses and]
23 [no] longer s[i]n."

FRAGMENT 2: Recto

1 [—].
2 coming to him poi[nted-]
3 ly questioning him, s[aying,]
4 "Teacher Jesus, we know that [from God]
5 you have come. For the things you do test[ify]
6 beyond all t[h]e prophets. [Therefore you tell]
7 us: Is it right to the king[s to giv-]
8 e what belongs to their rule? Shall [we pay th-]
9 em or no[t]?" And Jesus, knowing [the mi-]

10　nd [of]them, indignantly
11　said to [them], "Why do you call me [with mo]
12　uth you[r 'Te]acher,' no[t hear-]
13　ing what I say? well I[saiah about y-]
14　ou pr[o]phesied, saying, [people th-]
15　is with the [li]ps of th[em honor]
16　me, the [but hear]t of the[m far aw-]
17　ay from m[e. Va]inl[y me they worship]
18　command[ments—]

Verso

1　[......]in place [sh]ut away-
2　[.....] placed underneath invisibly
3　[......] the weight of it unweighed
4　[.....] And being confused tho-
5　[se as] to the strange question
6　[of him, while w]alking, Jesus stood
7　[upon the] bank of the Jo[rd]an
8　[riv]er, and stretchin[g the] han-
9　[d of hi]m, his right, [...]
10　[.....a]nd he sowe[d it upo]n the
11　[......] and then
12　[......] water.
13　[..........]. And [.] bef-
14　[ore them it br]ought forth [and] fruit
15　[..........]|many[......] for j-
16　[oy.................]

P.MERTON 51

DESCRIPTION

This single fragment of a codex, dated to the third century, has writing on both sides.[al] Its original editors treated it as a "Christian Fragment" and

---

al.　Rees, "51. Christian Fragment," in *A Descriptive Catalogue of the Greek Papyri*, 2:1.

noted its possible homiletic nature and interaction with Luke 6–7.[am] It is possible the original reading order was verso, recto;[an] but as this is impossible to verify, the papyrus is usually presented in the traditional recto, verso order.

CONTENT HIGHLIGHTS

The recto opens with text reminiscent of Luke 7:29. In the canonical context, this is after Jesus' testimony that John is the messenger proclaiming him, and that while John is the greatest of the prophets, the least among the kingdom is greater than John (Luke 7:24–28). The response to this in P.Merton 51 involves the people, and specifically the tax collectors, testifying to the righteousness of God and confessing their sins. Here the editors also note parallels to 1 John 1:9 and Matt 3:6.[ao] The likeness to Lukan material continues, with themes from Luke 7:30 making themselves evident. The response of the Pharisees[ap] is the opposite of the people and the tax collectors; they refuse the baptism of John and reject "the plan of God and the commandment of God."[aq] This is followed (in reconstruction, primarily) by a formulaic statement of God's rejection of them. At this point, the papyrus has a double vertical dot at the end of the line, which is typically read as a section break. From here there is a sentence of new material, largely reconstructed based on Luke 7:36, introducing a Pharisee who, in contrast to those who rejected Jesus, wanted to eat with Him.

As noted in most editions,[ar] the verso is easier to reconstruct than the recto. The text is similar to that of Luke 6:45 (lines 1–5) and Luke 6:46 (lines 6–7); these verses are used to assist in the reconstruction.[as] However, the order in P.Merton 51 reverses that of the canonical content: the evil fruit is mentioned first, followed by the good fruit.

---

am. Ibid,. 2:1–2.
an. Ibid., 2:1.
ao. Ibid., 2:3.
ap. However, note only reconstructions contain the word "Pharisee"; it is not contained in the extant portions of the papyrus.
aq. See also Mark 7:9.
ar. Rees, "51. Christian Fragment," 2:1; Ehrman and Pleše, The Apocryphal Gospels, 255.
as. Rees, "51. Christian Fragment," 2:3–4.

RELEVANCE FOR EXEGESIS

P.Merton 51 contains strong canonical parallels and references. The seemingly tight relationships of the recto with Luke 7:29-30, 36 and the verso with Luke 6:45-46 provide a witness to the manner in which these episodes were used and understood in the third century, and likely before. If the reconstructions properly represent the content of the original, the episode on the recto gives an example of the favorable response of the general public to Jesus, contrasted with the rejection of the religious leaders.

The episode on the verso, with its progression from evil fruit to good fruit,[at] leaves the reader/hearer with the thought of good fruit in mind before the condemnation of not doing what the Lord commands. Then, in an expansion unique to P.Merton 51, there appears to be similar condemnation for not hearing what the prophet proclaims. Both of these exhortations underscore the importance of obeying the commands of the Lord and the words of the prophet, equating these things with good fruit that is not destroyed.

TRANSLATION

Reading Translation

FRAGMENT 1: Recto. and upon hearing, all the people and the tax collectors declared God righteous, confessing their own sins. But the Pharisees were not baptized by John. And they rejected the plan of God and the commandment of God.... likewise God rejects them. But a Pharisee asked him [to eat] with him ...

Verso. [for the evil person, from] evil, produced evil fruit, as an evil tree produces from evil. And when you send out good things from the good treasure of the heart, its good fruit is not destroyed. Now you do not call me "Lord, Lord," and do not do what I say, or when the prophet speaks do you hear ...

---

at. Compare to the good to evil progression in Luke 6:45-46.

Line Translation

FRAGMENT 1: Recto

1   [and all the peo]ple and the tax collect[ors]
2   [upon hearing decl]ared God righteous,
3   [confessing] their own sins.
4   [But the Pharisees] were not baptized
5   [by John. And the pl]an of God
6   [and the commandment of G]od they rejected.
7   [... likewise God them] rejects.
8   [But a Pharisee asked him w]ith hi[m]

Verso

1   [ev]il, produc[ing evil fruit pro-]
2   [d]uced as from e[vil, an evil tr-]
3   ee. And when you send [out from the go-]
4   od treasure of th[e heart, good things not]
5   is destroy[ed good fruit]
6   [i]ts. Now not [you do call me "Lord, Lord,"]
7   [and] do not do [what I say or the pro-]
8   [phe]t when spe[aking do you hear ...]

P.OXY. 210

DESCRIPTION

P.Oxy. 210 is damaged, making its reconstruction difficult. However, it is relatively early (third century)[au] and considered by some to be a commentary or homily.[av] The fragment is long and slim, with writing on both sides. The verso contains more material and thus more opportunity for reconstruction.

---

au. Bernard P. Grenfell and Arthur S. Hunt, eds., "210. Early Christian Fragment," in *The Oxyrhynchus Papyri* (London: Egypt Exploration Fund, 1899), 2:9; Brent Landau and Stanley E. Porter, "Papyrus Oxyrhynchus 210: A New Translation and Introduction" in eds. Tony Burke and Brent Landau, *New Testament Apocrypha: More Noncanonical Scriptures* (Grand Rapids: Wm. B. Eerdmans, 2016) 109–124.
av. Ehrman and Pleše, *The Apocryphal Gospels*, 259.

CONTENT HIGHLIGHTS

Because the papyrus is so fragmentary, reconstruction is difficult.[aw] Only phrases, not even whole clauses, can be made out. Despite this, the recto mentions an angel at least twice (lines 5–6) so it may have some relationship with Matt 1:24. The verso, however, has more extant text and therefore can be scrutinized more deeply. It mentions "good fruit" (line 15) and "good tree" (line 16), likely with Jesus as the speaker. Therefore the papyrus may have some relationship with Matt 7:17–19; 12:33–35; Luke 6:43–44; which record episodes of Jesus using similar language.[ax] The text of the recto also includes phrases like "in the form of God" (line 19) and "as the image of him" (line 20), which evoke Pauline material, particularly Phil 2:6 (although see also similar language in 2 Cor 4:4 and Col 1:15).

RELEVANCE FOR EXEGESIS

Primarily relevant for exegesis are the Pauline themes of the image and form of God (lines 19–20; Phil 2:6) occurring together with what is likely Jesus speaking of the "good fruit" and the "good tree." If this material is similar to the canonical material (Matt 7:17–19; 12:33–35; Luke 6:43–44), the good tree is exemplary, set apart as proper and good, and the fruit that comes from it is good because it is produced by the good tree. Tying in the notion of Jesus as the image (Col 1:15) and form (Phil 2:6) of God, perhaps from Jesus Himself, is a new spin on the canonical material.

TRANSLATION

Reading Translation

FRAGMENT 1: Recto. … he is not able … But to remain … angel … about an angel … to us the … this … yet …

Verso. … good … he said … Father … good … good … God … but … Jesus and he will say … good bears … bears good … fruit of a good tree … the good. I

---

aw. Ibid. Note that Lührmann's transcription, which is used in Ehrman, is much different than that of Grenfell and Hunt, which is the basis of the transcription and translation in the present volume.

ax. The reconstruction of P.Merton 51 recto lines 3–5 also uses "good fruit" and "good tree."

am ... I am the image of ... in the form of God ... as the image of him ... to God, to God the ... to be ... visible ... of the ... that ... person ...

Line Translation

FRAGMENT 1: Recto

1   [...]
2   [...]
3   not he is abl[e]
4   [t]o remain But [...]
5   [...] angel [...]
6   [abo]ut an angel [...]
7   [...] to us the [...]
8   [...]
9   this [...]
10 yet [...]
11 [...]
12 [...]
13 [...]
14 [—]
15 [—]
16 [—]
17 [...]

Verso

1   [...]
2   [...]
3   [...]
4   [...] good [...]
5   [...] he said [...]
6   [...] Father [...]
7   [...] good [...]
8   [...]
9   [...]
10 good [...]
11 [...]

12 [...] God [...] but [...]
13 [...] Jesus [a]nd he will say [...]
14 [go]od [be]ars [...]
15 [b]ear[s g]ood [...]
16 [fr]uit of a tree good
17 [...] the good. I am [...]
18 [...]|| I am the image of
19 [...] in the form of God
20 [...] as the image of hi[m]
21 [...] to God, to God the [...]
22 [...] to be [...]
23 [...] visible [...]
24 [...] of the [...]
25 [...] that [...]
26 [...]
27 [...]
28 [...] person [...]
29 [—]

P.OXY. 840

DESCRIPTION

P.Oxy. 840 is a parchment leaf that dates to the third or fourth century,[ay] although Bovon allows for as late as the fifth century.[az] Swete notes that the text recorded on the parchment may have originated in the first half of the second century.[ba] While some have considered P.Oxy. 840 an amulet,[bb] Kruger's explanation of the fragment originating as a miniature codex makes the most sense.[bc] The parchment leaf itself is small, and has text

---

ay. Michael J. Kruger, "II. Papyrus Oxyrhynchus 840," in *Gospel Fragments*, ed. Thomas J. Kraus, Michael J. Kruger, and Tobias Nicklas, Oxford Early Christian Gospel Texts (Oxford: Oxford University Press, 2009), 123; Ehrman and Pleše, *The Apocryphal Gospels*, 267.

az. François Bovon, "Fragment Oxyrhynchus 840, Fragment of a Lost Gospel, Witness of an Early Christian Controversy over Purity," *JBL* 119 (2000): 706.

ba. H. B. Swete, *Two New Gospel Fragments* (Cambridge: Deighton, Bell & Co., 1908), 3.

bb. Bovon, "Fragment Oxyrhynchus 840," 706; Ehrman and Pleše, *The Apocryphal Gospels*, 267.

bc. Kruger, "II. Papyrus Oxyrhynchus 840," 125–127.

written on the front and back. At times it uses red ink to outline certain features such as punctuation and overlines. Kruger paints the picture of a scribe who was not an amateur, who may have been copying the manuscript for a wealthy individual.[bd] Further, the features of the manuscript imply that "by the time our scribe did his work the text had been in circulation for some time. It is unlikely that a recent composition, that had yet to achieve literary popularity, would warrant the creation of an expensive edition like P.Oxy. 840."[be]

CONTENT HIGHLIGHTS

P.Oxy. 840 tells the story of Jesus and his disciples going to "the place of purification" and entering into the temple. They are met by a chief priest who is also a Pharisee, named Levi. The priest questions them as to why they are in the temple, for the priest views Jesus and his disciples as defiled and impure. Jesus asks the priest if he is clean. The priest responds that he is, that he washed himself "in the pool of David," and then gives details of that structure. The priest also notes that after his washing he put on clean, white clothes. Jesus responds with a woe statement, condemning him for cleansing the outside without paying attention to the inside. Jesus says that he and his disciples are cleansed on the inside, that they "have been dipped in waters of eternal life." This is followed with a further woe statement, the text of which is lost.

While the text of P.Oxy. 840 reads easily enough, there are some issues with the content. First is the notion of a chief priest also being a Pharisee. This is difficult because chief priests were usually Sadducees.[bf] Second, the inclusion of "the place of purification" (ἀγνευτήριον, *hagneutērion*) and discussion of "the holy vessels" is problematic because the manner in which they are discussed does not easily align with current knowledge of such things.[bg] Lastly, mention of "the pool of David" is difficult because the temple complex as it is known today has no such pool.[bh]

---

bd. Ibid., 135–139.

be. Ibid., 139.

bf. Bovon, "Fragment Oxyrhynchus 840," 707; Kruger, "II. Papyrus Oxyrhynchus 840," 145–47.

bg. Kruger, "II. Papyrus Oxyrhynchus 840," 147–50; Bovon, "Fragment Oxyrhynchus 840," 707.

bh. Ibid., 150–53

These issues, however, are resolvable. Regarding a chief priest who was a Pharisee, there are some exceptions mentioned in Josephus and the Mishnah that appear to allow for this combination.[bi] Regarding the holy vessels and the place of purification, while such things were not typically visible from the outside of the temple, there were apparently times during certain feasts where the curtain of the temple was drawn back, and people could view the interior, including the holy vessels.[bj] It is possible that the episode described above was set during just such a celebration. Lastly, regarding the "pool of David" and its staircase entry and exit, Kruger notes the description fits that of a *mikveh*, a Jewish ritual bathing pool. He contends "divided stairways were in fact very common among stepped pools of the Second Temple Period, particularly in the area in and around Jerusalem—precisely the setting of our story in P.Oxy. 840."[bk]

Providing a resolution to these issues does not imply the account is genuine and factual, but it does lend credence to details of the account and allow for the story to be set within the time of Jesus.

RELEVANCE FOR EXEGESIS

Kruger, in his extensive essay on P.Oxy. 840, writes "... P.Oxy. 840 has clear verbal, structural, and thematic connections to five passages in the canonical gospels: Luke 11:37–52; Matt. 23:1–39; John 7:1–52; John 13:1–30; and Mark 7:1–23."[bl] The first two passages contain episodes of Jesus pronouncing woes against the Pharisees regarding the cleansing of the outside but not purifying the inside. In P.Oxy. 840, Jesus also pronounces woes against the Pharisees to similar effect.

A common theme in all the references cited by Kruger is that of purity. Bovon considers P.Oxy. 840 a window into a second-century controversy over purity,[bm] and it may be.[bn] When evaluating issues of ritual purity in the early church, P.Oxy. 840 should be evaluated because of its relationship with the gospels on issues of purity.

---

bi. Ibid., 146. See Josephus, *Life* 21; 197; *Wars* 2.410–11. For the Mishnah, see *m.Abot.* 3.2; *m.Pesah.* 1.6.

bj. Ibid., 149–50

bk. Ibid., 152

bl. Ibid., 157

bm. Bovon, "Fragment Oxyrhynchus 840."

bn. Hans-Josef Klauck, *Apocryphal Gospels: An Introduction* (London: T&T Clark, 2004), 27.

TRANSLATION

Reading Translation

FRAGMENT 1: Recto. ... previously, before unjust action he makes every crafty excuse. But pay attention, lest you also suffer the same things as them. For not only among the living do the evildoers receive their reward among people, but they also await punishment and great torment. And taking them he brought them into the very place of purification and walked in the temple. And a certain Pharisee, a high priest named Levi, came and met them and said to the Savior, "Who permitted you to walk in this place of purification and to see these holy vessels, neither having washed nor even have your disciples bathed their feet? But having been defiled you have walked in this temple, a place being pure, where no one else who has not washed and changed his clothes walks, neither dares to see these holy vessels." And the Savior immediately stood still with his disciples, answering to him,

Verso. "You, then, being here in the temple, are you clean?" That one said to him, "I am clean. For I washed in the pool of David and I came down by another staircase, and went up by another, and put on white and clean clothes, and then went and looked upon these holy vessels." Answering, the Savior said to him, "Woe to you, blind ones who do not see. You have washed in these running waters in which dogs and pigs have been cast night and day, and have cleansed the outsides of your skin, which also the prostitutes and the flute-girls anoint and wash and scrub and beautify for the lust of men. But those ones are filled inside with scorpions and every evil. But I and my disciples, who you say have not bathed, have been dipped in waters of eternal life which come from ... But woe to those ..."

Line Translation

FRAGMENT 1: Recto

1   previously, before unjust action he makes every crafty ex-
2   cuse. But pay attention, lest also
3   you the same things as them suffer. For not

4   among only the living do receive their re-
5   ward the evildoers among people, but [a]lso
6   punishment they await and gre[a]t
7   torment. And taking them
8   he brought them into the very place of purification and
9   walked in the temple. And came
10   a certain Pharisee, a high priest Le[vi]
11   named met them and s[ai]d
12   to the Sav[io]r, "Who gave permission to you to walk
13   in this place of purification and to see [the-]
14   se holy vessels, neither having washed n[o-]
15   r even your disciples f[eet ba-]
16   thed? But having been defiled
17   you have walked in this temple, a pl[ace be-]
18   ing pure, where no one el[se if not]
19   being washed and chang[ed his clo-]
20   thes walks, neither to [see dares these]
21   holy vessels." And stood st[ill immediately the Savior]
22   w[ith h]is disciple[s, answering to him,]

Verso

23   "You, then, being here in the temple, are you
24   clean?" That one said to him, "I am clean. I was-
25   hed For in the pool of David and by anoth-
26   er staircase I came down, by another
27   we[n]t up, and white clothes put
28   on and clean, and then went
29   and looked upon these holy
30   vessels." The Savior to him ans-
31   [wer]ing said, "Woe to you, blind ones who do not s-
32   e[e]. You have washed in these running
33   w[a]ters in which dogs and pigs have been ca-
34   [st] night and day, and have cleans-
35   [e]d the outsides of your skin, which
36   [al]so the prostitutes and th[e] flute-girls anoi-
37   [n]t [a]nd wash and scrub

38 [and b]eautify for the lus-

39 [t o]f men. within But those

40 [ones are fi]lled with scorpions and

41 [every ev]il. I But and the

42 [disciples my] who you say not have bath-

43 [thed, have been] dipped in waters of li-

44 [fe eternal whic]h come from. [.]

45 [........B]ut woe to [t]hose [...]

P.OXY. 1224

DESCRIPTION

Grenfell and Hunt date P.Oxy. 1224 to the fourth century.[bo] It includes two fragments: one small and one relatively large. Fragment one is too small for any reliable reconstruction.[bp] Both fragments preserve the upper portions of a manuscript and what appear to be page numbers. The ordering of the columns of the second fragment, however, is in dispute. Most transcriptions and translations follow the order of Grenfell and Hunt, who proposed the two columns on the recto and verso of fragment two were pages in a bifolio edition, with the numbering indicating an order resembling what we today would see as a pamphlet, with the papyrus folded in the middle, forming four pages.[bq] However, based on the extant page numbers (139, 174 and 176; the others are reconstructed), the codex is sizeable and not simply a four-page pamphlet. The pages were not large, and likely had 20 lines at most.[br]

If P.Oxy. 1224 is a noncanonical gospel, then from the available material (which appears to be but a sliver of the whole codex) it appears to focus on Jesus' interactions with those around him instead of events in his life.

---

bo. Grenfell and Hunt, "1224. Uncanonical Gospel," in *The Oxyrhynchus Papyri* (London: Egypt Exploration Fund, 1914), 10:1.

bp. Ibid, 10:2.

bq. Ibid, 10:1-2; Thomas J. Kraus, "5. P.Oxy. 1224," in *Gospel Fragments*, ed. Thomas J. Kraus, Michael J. Kruger, and Tobias Nicklas, Oxford Early Christian Gospel Texts (Oxford: Oxford University Press, 2009), 265-66.

br. Grenfell and Hunt, "1224. Uncanonical Gospel," 10:2.

Some also discuss the possibility that it could be a sayings gospel akin to Thomas, but there is too little material available to make this judgment.[bs]

Content Highlights

The content of the first fragment is scant and impossible to reconstruct outside of the formulaic statement, "truly I say to you." If the page number (139) is correct, then it is more than 30 pages removed from the material of fragment two.

As fragment 2 includes the top five to six lines (of possibly 20 lines per page)[bt] of four consecutive columns, it is essentially four consecutive fragmentary portions of the manuscript. While each portion of the content involves some sort of interaction with Jesus, there is not enough connection between the columns, outside of the remains of page numbers, for a coherent reconstruction of the whole fragment.

The first portion of fragment 2, page 173, includes Jesus appearing in a vision, addressing the discouragement of the one he appears to. The next portion, page 174, looks to be an inquiry of Jesus, asking about his new teaching (compare Mark 1:27). The next portion, likely page 175, relates an episode of Jesus "reclining in the midst of sinners," responding to the criticism of the scribes, Pharisees and priests about how "[t]he healthy have no need of a doctor." It appears to be an abridgment of Mark 2:16–17, Matt 9:11–12; Luke 5:30–31.[bu] The final portion, page 176, is also a dialogue of Jesus, including some wisdom statements: "pray for your enemies" (lines 1–2; compare Matt 5:44; Luke 6:27–28; *Did.* 1.3);[bv] "he who is not with you is against you" (lines 2–3; compare Mark 9:40; Luke 9:50; slightly different form in Matt 12:30).[bw]

Relevance for Exegesis

The fragmentary nature notwithstanding, P.Oxy. 1224 has several points of contact with the canonical Gospels. The portions making up pages 175 and 176 contain material that is also witnessed in the Synoptic Gospels,

---

bs. Ibid., 10:1–3; Kraus, "5. P.Oxy. 1224," 279.

bt. Grenfell and Hunt, "1224. Uncanonical Gospel," 10:2.

bu. Kraus, "5. P.Oxy. 1224," 273.

bv. Ibid.

bw. Ibid.

although in different forms. Page 175 is also important in grouping together, if the reconstruction is correct, "scribes and Pharisees and priests." This grouping is not commonly seen in the New Testament.

However, there are some divergences. One portion, page 173, has Jesus appearing in a vision offering consolation. There are no equivalent episodes in the canonical Gospels, although perhaps a post-resurrection appearance could be construed this way. Page 174 mentions "new teaching" and "new baptism" (if the reconstruction is correct). Such language is not unknown to the Gospels (compare Mark 1:27) but it is not frequent either.

At minimum, P.Oxy. 1224 shows the author had basic familiarity with the canonical texts and other material about Jesus. The author knew and used wisdom statements of Jesus, and retold portions of Jesus' story to his audience.

TRANSLATION

Reading Translation

FRAGMENT 1: Recto. 139 ... in all.... Truly I say to you ...

Verso. ... you ...

FRAGMENT 2: Recto Column 2. 173 ... he overcame me. And Jesus stood by in a vision. He said, "Why are you discouraged? For not ... you but the ...

Verso Column 1. 174 ... you spoke without answering. What then have you spoken? What new teaching do they say you teach, or what new baptism do you preach? Answer and ...

Verso Column 2. 175 ... But the scribes and Pharisees and priests, upon seeing him, became indignant because he was reclining in the midst of sinners. But Jesus, upon hearing, said "The healthy have no need of a doctor...."

Recto Column 1. 176 ... And pray for your enemies. For he who is not with you is against you. The one who is far away today will be near you tomorrow, and in ... of the adversary ...

Line Translation

FRAGMENT 1: Recto

1   139
2   [...]in all
3   [.........]. Truly to y-
4   [ou I say]
5   [...]

Verso

1
2   .. you [.........]
3   [.]. [.........]
4   [...]

FRAGMENT 2: Recto Column 2

1   1 [73]
2   me he overcame. And [stood]
3   by Jesus [i]n a visio[n, he said]
4   "Why are you dis[cour]aged? For not [........]
5   [y]ou but the [..............]
6   [...]

Verso Column 1

1   174
2   [you] said not answer-
3   [ing. What then have you] spoken? W[h]at you
4   [they say teach]ing ne[w] you
5   [teach, or what b]a[ptis]m new
6   [do you preach? Answ]er and

Verso Column 2

1   [175]
2   But the scribes an[d Pharis-]
3   ees and priests, upon see[ing hi-]
4   m be]came indignant [because with sin-]

5 ers in the mi[dst he was reclining.]

6 But Jesus, upon hearing, [he said "No need]

7 [h]ave the healthy

8 [of a doctor].[...]

9 [...]

Recto Column 1

1 [1]76

2 [A]nd p[r]ay for

3 [the ene]mies of you, For he not being

4 [with yo]u against you is.

5 [The one today bei]ng far away tomorrow

6 [near you wi]ll be, and in

7 [...........]. of the advers[ary]

8 [.............].....[...]

9 [...]

P.OXY. 5072

DESCRIPTION

P.Oxy. 5072 is dated to the end of the second or beginning of the third century.[bx] It is a small fragment with writing on both sides, and was likely part of a codex. Chapa reports some similarities between P.Oxy. 5072 and both P.Egerton 2 and P.Oxy. 1224.[by] The transcription is based on available images,[bz] in consultation with Chapa's published description.[ca] The transcription includes some reconstruction, but only that which is in agreement with Chapa, with notes on reconstructions that Chapa includes but this transcription does not.

---

bx. J. Chapa, "5072. Uncanonical Gospel?," in *The Oxyrhynchus Papyri*, ed. J. Chapa and D. Colomo (London: Egypt Exploration Society, 2012), 76:1; Ross P. Ponder, "Papyrus Oxyrhynchus 5072: A New Translation and Introduction" in eds. Tony Burke and Brent Landau, *New Testament Apocrypha: More Noncanonical Scriptures* (Grand Rapids: Wm. B. Eerdmans, 2016) 125–139.

by. Ibid., 76:6–7.

bz. *POxy: Oxyrhynchus Online*, http://www.papyrology.ox.ac.uk/POxy/

ca. Chapa, "5072. Uncanonical Gospel?" 76:1–19.

CONTENT HIGHLIGHTS

The recto of the fragment contains an account of Jesus[cb] casting out a demon. It records portions of a conversation between the demon and Jesus. There are mentions of the demon-possessed man (?) tearing something apart (his clothes, or perhaps chains as in Mark 5:4), then crying out to the "son,"[cc] protesting "have you come before the time." The demon speaking through the man is then rebuked and cast out. The scene then switches, but not enough text remains to determine the next scene.

The verso appears to be a dialogue involving Jesus.[cd] If the speaker is Jesus, and this appears to be the best assumption, the account has Jesus noting he will deny the one being spoken to. This appears to be most similar to Luke 12:8–9; but has contact with Matt 10:32–33 and Mark 8:38.[ce] The next few lines appear to define who is and is not a disciple of Jesus through an account that has some similarity with Luke 14:26–27.[cf]

RELEVANCE FOR EXEGESIS

P.Oxy. 5072 has several points of contact with Synoptic material. The story of the demon-possessed man, similar to the accounts of the demoniac in Mark 5:7–13; Matt 8:28–32; and Luke 8:26–33, confirms that stories of Jesus casting out demons were still found valuable in the second and third centuries. Of the entire exchange, Chapa notes:

> Thus, it seems reasonable to think that on this side we are dealing with a narrative which was inspired by accounts of exorcism recorded in the New Testament, and specifically by the three most developed episodes: the possessed man at the synagogue of Capharnaum, the demoniac(s) at the lake of Gennesaret, and the healing of the lunatic boy.[cg]

---

cb. While Jesus is not explicitly mentioned in the available material, the stories only make sense with Jesus as the primary actor. Chapa's reconstruction does read I(ησου)ς at the start of recto line 9.

cc. Likely υιε του θεου, "Son of God!" which is used in the synoptic parallels.

cd. Chapa, "5072. Uncanonical Gospel?" 76:4–5.

ce. Ibid., 76:5.

cf. Ibid.

cg. J. Chapa, "A newly published 'gospel fragment'," *Early Christianity* 3, no. 3 (September 2012): 385.

The portions available on the verso, having to do with whom Jesus will accept or deny, appear to synthesize synoptic material on the same topic (Luke 12:8–9; Matt 10:23–33; Mark 8:38). The material is expressive, with Jesus noting "I myself will deny," and his addressee being "shamefully" treated in some way. Further discussion involves who is and who is not a true disciple, recalling Luke 14:26–27. There is possible mention of scribes, Jerusalem, and the kingdom,[ch] and even perhaps some talk of keeping things "hidden" from the intelligent. While no gospel accounts contain all these topics in such a compact space, these concepts are known in Jesus' teaching. Hiding things from the intelligent is a notion found in Matt 11:25 and Luke 10:21. Jerusalem and the kingdom occur together in Luke 19:11. These perhaps show some preference for the vocabulary of Luke,[ci] but they certainly indicate the author's desire to convey teaching, using synoptic accounts and vocabulary, about the nature of true disciples.

TRANSLATION

Reading Translation

FRAGMENT 1: Recto. ... before ... but he tore apart as much as ... he cried out, saying, "Son ... have you come before the time us ...?" ... he rebuked him, saying, "... go out from the man ..." ... going he sat down ... of them ... Jesus ... someone to him ...

Verso. ... a teacher, but I myself will deny you ... of my disciple and you will be shamefully ... last things. Yes, I say to you, friend ... of him more than me, he is not ... disciple. If then scribes ... Jerusalem and if ... and Kingdom ... before you ... intelligent he kept hidden ... disciples ...

Line Translation

FRAGMENT 1: Recto

1   [...]before [...]

---

ch. Here "kingdom" is a nomina sacra, $\beta\alpha(\sigma\iota)\lambda\varepsilon\iota\alpha$.
ci. Chapa, "5072. Uncanonical Gospel?," 76:5–6.

2 [...] but he tore apart as much as [...]

3 [...] he cried out, saying, Son [...]

4 [... have] you come before the time us.[...]

5 [...]he rebuked him, say[ing ...]

6 [... go] out from the man[...]

7 [...].going he sat down.[...]

8 [... of] them [...]

9 [... Jesu]s [...]

10 [...][...]

11 [...] someone to him [...]

Verso

1 [...].[...]

2 [...].[...]...[...]

3 [... a] teacher, myself but you I will [deny ...]

4 [... of] my disciple and you will be shame[fully ...]

5 [... las]t things. Yes, I say to you, fr[iend ...]

6 [. of] him more than me, not he [is ...]

7 [... dis]ciple. If then scrib[es ...]

8 [...]Jerusalem and if [...]

9 [...]. [...] and Kingdom [...]

10 [... be]fore yo[u ...]

11 [... inte]lligent he kept hid[den ...]

12 [... d]isciples [...]

13 [...].[...]

P.VINDOBONENSIS G.2325

DESCRIPTION

P.Vindobonensis G.2325, sometimes called the "Fayûm Fragment," is a small papyrus with text only on the verso. This indicates it may have been part of a roll.[cj] Kraus notes that the papyrus likely "dates from the third century,

---

cj. C. Wessely, "Fragments de collections de prétendues sentences de Jésus," in *Les plus anciens monuments du christianisme écrits sur papyrus*, Patrologia Orientalis 4.2 (Paris: Firmin-Didot, 1906), 173; Thomas J. Kraus, "1. P.Vindob.G 2325: 'The Fayûm Fragment'," in *Gospel Fragments*, 219.

perhaps towards the beginning."[ck] Wessely notes the papyrus was found in a layer of material from Heracleopolis,[cl] which is in Middle Egypt, in the southeast Fayûm.[cm] The transcription is that of Wessely.[cn]

One peculiarity of this papyrus is the representation of Peter's name. It is an abbreviation, a nomina sacra, and the text is in red ink instead of the black used for the rest of the text.[co] This has led some to suggest that the papyrus is a fragment of the Gospel of Peter,[cp] although this view has not been widely accepted.[cq]

CONTENT HIGHLIGHTS

The papyrus opens with an episode from the night of Jesus' arrest. It witnesses material found in Mark 14:26–30 and Matt 26:30–34. Jesus is warning his disciples that they will fall away that very night, with the further warning to Peter (after his protest) that he will deny Jesus three times before the rooster crows twice.

RELEVANCE FOR EXEGESIS

The content of P. Vindobonensis G.2325 has strong parallels in two canonical Gospels, Matt 26:30–34; Mark 14:26–30; and looser parallels in the other two: Luke 22:34; John 13:38. It also records the quotation of Zech 13:7 found in Matthew and Mark. However, Jesus is not explicitly referred to at the beginning of the material. The quotation from Zech 13:7 is introduced a bit differently. There is no mention of the disciples meeting Jesus in Galilee after Jesus' resurrection (Mark 14:28; Matt 26:32).

The vocabulary and phrasing of Jesus' pronouncement regarding the rooster is also different from the canonical versions. A different word for "rooster" is used; this one is more common in classical texts and less

---

ck. Kraus, "1. P.Vindob.G 2325," 220.

cl. Wessely, "Fragments de collections de prétendues sentences de Jésus," 173.

cm. Kraus, "1. P.Vindob.G 2325," 220.

cn. Wessely, "Fragments de collections de prétendues sentences de Jésus," 176–177.

co. Kraus, "1. P.Vindob.G 2325," 219.

cp. D. Lührmann and E. Schlarb, *Fragmente apokryph gewordener Evangelien in Griechischer und lateinischer Sprache*, Marburger theologische Studien 59 (Marburg: N. G. Elwert, 2000), 73–81.

cq. Kraus, "1. P.Vindob.G 2325," 225.

common "in the vernacular Greek of the first three centuries."[cr] A different verb for "to crow" is also used.[cs]

TRANSLATION

Reading Translation

FRAGMENT 1: Recto. [blank]

Verso. ... and he brought out, as he said, that "In this night you will all fall away, as it is written: 'I will strike the shepherd and the sheep will be scattered.'" Peter said, "Even if everyone else does, I will not." Jesus said, "Before the rooster crows twice, today you will deny me three times."

Line Translation

FRAGMENT 1: Recto. [blank]

Verso

1   [and he b]rought out, as he s[a]i[d], that "a[ll]
2   [in this] night you will fall [awa-]
3   [y, as] it is written: 'I will strike the [shep-]
4   [herd and the] sheep will be scatte[red.'" Sa-]
5   [id] Peter, "Even if everyone, n[ot I." Sa-]
6   [id Jesus, "Be]fore the rooster twice cro[ws, thrice]
7   [you today me will] d[eny.]

SELECT BIBLIOGRAPHY

Bell, Sir Harold I., and T. C. Skeat, eds. *Fragments of an Unknown Gospel and Other Early Christian Papyri.* New impression. London: British Museum Press, 1935.

Bernhard, Andrew. *Other Early Christian Gospels: A Critical Edition of the Surviving Greek Manuscripts.* London: T&T Clark, 2007.

---

cr. Ibid., 224.
cs. Ibid.

Bovon, François. "Fragment Oxyrhynchus 840, Fragment of a Lost
    Gospel, Witness of an Early Christian Controversy over Purity."
    Journal of Biblical Literature 119 (2000): 705–28.

Chapa, J. "5072. Uncanonical Gospel?" Pages 1–19 in Vol. 76 of *The
    Oxyrhynchus Papyri*. Edited by J. Chapa and D. Colomo. London:
    Egypt Exploration Society, 2012.

———. "A newly published 'gospel fragment'." *Early Christianity* 3, no. 3
    (September 2012): 381–89.

Deissmann, Adolf. *Light from the Ancient East: The New Testament
    Illustrated by Recently Discovered Texts of the Graeco-Roman World*.
    Translated by Lionel Richard Mortimer Strachan. London:
    Hodder & Stoughton, 1910.

Ehrman, Bart D., and Zlatko Pleše. *The Apocryphal Gospels: Texts and
    Translations*. Oxford: Oxford University Press, 2010.

Goodspeed, E. J., and I. A. Sparks. "Papyrus." *ISBE* 3:651–55.

Grenfell, Bernard P., and Arthur S. Hunt. "1224. Uncanonical Gospel."
    Pages 1–10 in Vol. 10 of *The Oxyrhynchus Papyri*. London: Egypt
    Exploration Fund, 1914.

———, eds. "210. Early Christian Fragment." Pages 9–10 in Vol. 2 of *The
    Oxyrhynchus Papyri*. London: Egypt Exploration Fund, 1899.

———. *Catalogue Général des Antiquitiés Égyptiennes du Musée du Caire,
    Nos. 10001–10869: Greek Papyri*. Oxford: University Press, 1903.

Gronewald, Michael. "255. Unbekanntes Evangelium oder
    Evangelienharmonie (Fragment aus dem Evangelium Egerton)."
    Pages 136–45 in Vol. 6 of *Kölner Papyri*. Edited by Michael
    Gronewald, B. Kramer, K. Maresch, M. Parca, and C. Römer.
    Opladen: Westdeutscher Verlag, 1987.

James, M. R. *The Apocryphal New Testament*. Oxford: Clarendon, 1924.

Klauck, Hans-Josef. *Apocryphal Gospels: An Introduction*. London: T&T
    Clark, 2004.

Kraeling, Carl H. *A Greek Fragment of Tatian's Diatessaron from Dura:
    Edited with Facsimile, Transcription, and Introduction*. Studies and
    Documents 3. London: Christophers, 1935.

Kraus, Thomas J. "1. P.Vindob.G 2325: 'The Fayûm Fragment'." Pages
    219–27 in *Gospel Fragments*. Edited by Thomas J. Kraus, Michael J.

Kruger, and Tobias Nicklas. Oxford Early Christian Gospel Texts. Oxford: Oxford University Press, 2009.

⸻. "2. P.Berol 11710." Pages 228–39 in *Gospel Fragments*. Edited by Thomas J. Kraus, Michael J. Kruger, and Tobias Nicklas. Oxford Early Christian Gospel Texts. Oxford: Oxford University Press, 2009.

⸻. "3. P.Cair.G 10735." Pages 240–51 in *Gospel Fragments*. Edited by Thomas J. Kraus, Michael J. Kruger, and Tobias Nicklas. Oxford Early Christian Gospel Texts. Oxford: Oxford University Press, 2009.

⸻. "5. P.Oxy. 1224." Pages 264–80 in *Gospel Fragments*. Edited by Thomas J. Kraus, Michael J. Kruger, and Tobias Nicklas. Oxford Early Christian Gospel Texts. Oxford: Oxford University Press, 2009.

⸻. "Reconstructing Fragmentary Manuscripts—Chances and Limitations." Pages 1–38 in *Early Christian Manuscripts*. Edited by T. J. Kraus and T. Nicklas. Texts and Editions for New Testament Study 5. Leiden: Brill, 2010.

Kruger, Michael J. "II. Papyrus Oxyrhynchus 840." Pages 123–215 in *Gospel Fragments*. Edited by Thomas J. Kraus, Michael J. Kruger, and Tobias Nicklas. Oxford Early Christian Gospel Texts. Oxford: Oxford University Press, 2009.

Landau, Brent and Stanley E. Porter, "Papyrus Oxyrhynchus 210: A New Translation and Introduction." Pages 109–124 in *New Testament Apocrypha: More Noncanonical Scriptures*. Edited by Tony Burke and Brent Landau. Grand Rapids: Wm. B. Eerdmans, 2016.

Lietzmann, H. "Ein apokryphes Evangelienfragment." *Zeitschrift für die neutestamentliche Wissenschaft und die Kunde der älteren Kirche* 22 (1923): 153–54.

Lührmann, D., and E. Schlarb. *Fragmente apokryph gewordener Evangelien in Griechischer und lateinischer Sprache*. Marburger theologische Studien 59. Marburg: N. G. Elwert, 2000.

Nicklas, Tobias. "I. The 'Unknown Gospel' on Papyrus Egerton 2 (+ Papyrus Cologne 255)." Pages 11–120 in *Gospel Fragments*. Edited by Thomas J. Kraus, Michael J. Kruger, and Tobias Nicklas. Oxford

Early Christian Gospel Texts. Oxford: Oxford University Press, 2009.

Parker, D. C., D. K. G. Taylor, and M. S. Goodacre. "The Dura-Europos Gospel Harmony." Pages 192–228 in *Studies in the Early Text of the Gospels and Acts: The Papers of the First Birmingham Colloquium on the Textual Criticism of the New Testament*. Edited by D. K. G. Taylor. Text-Critical Studies. Atlanta: Society of Biblical Literature, 1999.

Ponder, Ross P., "Papyrus Oxyrhynchus 5072: A New Translation and Introduction." Pages 125–139 in <italic>New Testament Apocrypha: More Noncanonical Scriptures</italic>. Edited by Tony Burke and Brent Landau. Grand Rapids: Wm. B. Eerdmans, 2016.

Ponder, Ross P., "Papyrus Oxyrhynchus 5072: A New Translation and Introduction." Pages 125–139 in *New Testament Apocrypha: More Noncanonical Scriptures*. Edited by Tony Burke and Brent Landau. Grand Rapids: Wm. B. Eerdmans, 2016.

Rees, B. R. "51. Christian Fragment." Pages 1–4 in Vol. 2 of *A Descriptive Catalogue of the Greek Papyri in the Collection of Wilfred Merton, F.S.A.* Edited by B. R. Rees, Sir Harold I. Bell, and J. W. B. Barns. 3 vols. Merton Papyri. Dublin: Hodges Figgis, 1959.

Schneemelcher, Wilhelm, ed. *New Testament Apocrypha*. Rev. ed. Translated by R. McL. Wilson. 2 vols. Louisville: Westminster John Knox, 1991.

Sparks, I. A. "Parchment." *ISBE* 3:663.

Swete, H. B. *Two New Gospel Fragments*. Cambridge: Deighton, Bell & Co., 1908.

Wessely, C. "Fragments de collections de prétendues sentences de Jésus." Pages 151–82 in *Les plus anciens monuments du christianisme écrits sur papyrus*. Patrologia Orientalis 4.2. Paris: Firmin-Didot, 1906.

— *Bibliography*

The bibliography below contains entries in the following categories:

- Apocryphal Gospels (General)

- Agrapha

- Infancy Gospels

- Passion Gospels

- Post-Resurrection Gospels

- Fragments

APOCRYPHAL GOSPELS (GENERAL)

Bernhard, Andrew. *Other Early Christian Gospels: A Critical Edition of the Surviving Greek Manuscripts*. London: T&T Clark, 2007.

Bovon, François. *New Testament and Christian Apocrypha*. Edited by Glenn E. Snyder. Grand Rapids: Baker Academic, 2009.

Bromiley, Geoffrey W., ed. *The International Standard Bible Encyclopedia [ISBE]*. Rev. ed. 4 vols. Grand Rapids: Eerdmans, 1979–1988.

Ehrman, Bart D., and Zlatko Pleše. *The Apocryphal Gospels: Texts and Translations*. Oxford: Oxford University Press, 2010.

Elliott, J. K., ed. *The Apocryphal New Testament: A Collection of Apocryphal Christian Literature in an English Translation*. Oxford: Oxford University Press, 1994.

Evans, Craig A. *Ancient texts for New Testament Studies: A Guide to the Background Literature*. Peabody, MA: Hendrickson, 2005.

———. "The Life of Jesus." Pages 427–75 in *Handbook to the Exegesis of the New Testament*. Edited by S. E. Porter. New Testament Tools and Studies 25. Leiden: Brill, 1997.

Foster, Paul. *The Apocryphal Gospels: A Very Short Introduction*. Very Short Introductions 201. Oxford: Oxford University Press, 2009.

Freedman, David Noel, ed. *The Anchor Bible Dictionary* [ABD]. 6 vols. New York: Doubleday, 1992.

Hedrick, Charles W. *The Historical Jesus and the Rejected Gospels*. Semeia 44. Atlanta: Scholars Press, 1988.

Herbert, Máire, and Martin McNamera. *Irish Biblical Apocrypha: Selected Texts in Translation*. London: T&T Clark, 2004.

James, M. R. *Apocrypha anecdota: A Collection of Thirteen Apocryphal Books and Fragments*. Texts and Studies 2. Cambridge: Cambridge University Press, 1893.

———. *Apocrypha anecdota. Second Series*. Texts and Studies 5. Cambridge: Cambridge University Press, 1893.

———. *The Apocryphal New Testament*. Oxford: Clarendon, 1924.

Klauck, Hans-Josef. *Apocryphal Gospels: An Introduction*. London: T&T Clark, 2004.

Koester, Helmut. *Ancient Christian Gospels: Their History and Development*. Philadelphia: Trinity Press International, 1990.

Lapham, Fred. *Introduction to the New Testament Apocrypha*. London: T&T Clark, 2003.

Meier, John P. "Sources: The Agrapha and the Apocryphal Gospels." Pages 112–66 in *The Roots of the Problem and the Person*. Vol. 1 of *A Marginal Jew: Rethinking the Historical Jesus*. 4 vols. Anchor Bible Reference Library. New York: Doubleday, 1991.

Moreschini, Claudio, and Enrico Norelli. *Early Christian Greek and Latin Literature: A Literary History*. Peabody, MA: Hendrickson, 2005.

Porter, S. E. "The Greek Apocryphal Gospels Papyri: The Need for a Critical Edition." Pages 795–803 in Vol. 2 of *Akten des 21. Internationalen Papyrologenkongresses: Berlin, 13.–19.8.1995*. Edited by B. Kramer, W. Luppe, H. Maehler, and G. Poethke. Stuttgart: B. G. Teubner, 1997.

Ramos, Alex. "Apocryphal Gospels." In *Lexham Bible Dictionary*. Edited by John D. Barry, et al. Bellingham, WA: Logos Bible Software, 2012–2015.

Santos Otero, A. de. *Los Evangelios apócrifos: Colección de textos griegos y latinos, versión crítica, estudios introductorios y comentarios*. Rev. ed. Madrid: Biblioteca de Autores Cristianos, 2003.

Schneemelcher, Wilhelm, ed. *New Testament Apocrypha*. Rev. ed. Translated by R. McL. Wilson. 2 vols. Louisville: Westminster John Knox, 1991.

Tischendorf, C. von. *Evangelia Apocrypha*. 2nd ed. Leipzig: Mendelssohn, 1876.

AGRAPHA

Baker, A. "Justin's Agraphon in the Dialogue with Trypho." *Journal of Biblical Literature* 87 (1968): 277–87.

Bellinzoni, Arthur J. *The sayings of Jesus in the writings of Justin Martyr*. Supplements to Novum Testamentum. Leiden: E. J. Brill, 1967.

Brannan, Rick. "Apostolic Fathers." In *Lexham Bible Dictionary*. Edited by John D. Barry, et al. Bellingham, WA: Logos Bible Software, 2012–2015.

———. *The Apostolic Fathers in English*. Bellingham, WA: Lexham Press, forthcoming.

Confraternity of Christian Doctrine, Board of Trustees, Catholic Church, National Conference of Catholic Bishops, and United States Catholic Conference. *The New American Bible: Translated from the Original Languages with Critical Use of All the Ancient Sources and Revised New Testament*. Washington D.C.: Confraternity of Christian Doctrine, 1996.

Cross, F. L., and E. A. Livingstone, eds. *The Oxford Dictionary of the Christian Church*. 3rd rev. ed. Oxford: Oxford University Press, 2005.

Crossan, J. D. *Sayings Parallels: A Workbook for the Jesus Tradition*. Philadelphia: Fortress, 1986.

Delobel, J. "The Sayings of Jesus in the Textual Tradition: Variant Readings in the Greek Manuscripts of the Gospels." Pages 431–57 in *Logia; Les Paroles de Jésus [The Sayings of Jesus]*. Edited by J. Delobel. Leuven: Peeters, 1982.

Dodd, John Theodore. *Sayings ascribed to Our Lord by the Fathers and other Primitive Writers and Incidents in His Life narrated by them, otherwise than found in Scripture*. Oxford: James Parker and Co., 1874.

Donfried, Karl Paul. *The Setting of Second Clement in Early Christianity*. Novum Testamentum Supplements 38. Leiden: Brill, 1974.

Erbetta, A. *Apocrifi del NT*. Casale Monferrato: Marietti, 1975.

Evans, Craig A. *Mark 8:27–16:20*. Edited by Ralph P. Martin and Lynn A. Losie. WBC 34B. Nashville: Thomas Nelson, 2001.

Fitzmyer, J. A. *The Acts of the Apostles: A New Translation with Introduction and Commentary*. Anchor Bible 31. New York: Doubleday, 1998.

———. *The Gospel According to Luke I—IX: Introduction, Translation, and Notes*. Anchor Bible 28. Garden City, NY: Doubleday, 1970.

Grant, Robert M. "Justin Martyr." *ABD* 3:1133–34.

Grant, Robert M., and Holt H. Graham. *First and Second Clement*. The Apostolic Fathers: A New Translation and Commentary 2. New York: Thomas Nelson & Sons, 1965.

Harris III, W. Hall, Elliot Ritzema, Rick Brannan, Douglas Mangum, Jeffrey A. Reimer, and Micah Wierenga, eds. *The Lexham English Bible*. Bellingham, WA: Logos Bible Software, 2012.

Hofius, O. "Isolated Sayings of the Lord." Pages 88–91 in Vol. 1 of *New Testament Apocrypha*. Rev. ed. Edited by Wilhelm Schneemelcher. Translated by R. McL. Wilson. 2 vols. Louisville: Westminster John Knox, 1991.

———. "Unknown Sayings of Jesus." Pages 336–60 in *The Gospel and the Gospels*. Edited by P. Stuhlmacher. Grand Rapids: Eerdmans, 1991.

Holmes, Michael W. *The Apostolic Fathers: Greek texts and English translations*. Grand Rapids: Baker Academic, 2007.

———, ed. *The Greek New Testament: SBL Edition*. Bellingham, WA: Logos Bible Software and the Society of Biblical Literature, 2010.

Jeremias, Joachim. *Unknown Sayings of Jesus*. Translated by Reginald H. Fuller. Eugene, OR: Wipf & Stock, 2008.

Koester, Helmut. *Synoptische Überlieferung bei den apostolische Vätern*. Berlin: Akademie Verlag, 1957.

———. "The Extracanonical Sayings of the Lord as Products of the Christian Community." Pages 57–77 in *The Historical Jesus and the Rejected Gospels*. Edited by Charles W. Hedrick. Semeia 44. Atlanta: Scholars Press, 1988.

Kraft, Robert A. *The Didache and Barnabas*. The Apostolic Fathers: A New Translation and Commentary 3. New York: Thomas Nelson & Sons, 1965.

Lake, Kirsopp, trans. *The Apostolic Fathers*. LCL 24. Cambridge, MA: Harvard University Press, 1912.

———. *The Apostolic Fathers*. LCL 25. Cambridge, MA: Harvard University Press, 1912.

Leanza, S. *I detti extracanonici de Gesù*. Messina: n.p., 1977.

Lightfoot, J. B. *The Apostolic Fathers Part 1, S. Clement of Rome*. 2 vols. 2nd ed. London: Macmillan, 1890.

Metzger, Bruce M., ed. *A Textual Commentary on the Greek New Testament*. 2nd rev. ed. New York: United Bible Societies, 1994.

Oxford Society of Historical Theology. *The New Testament in the Apostolic Fathers*. Oxford: Oxford University Press, 1905.

Patterson, Stephen J. "Logia." *ABD* 4:347–48.

Pick, Bernhard. *Paralipomena: Remains of Gospels and Sayings of Christ*. Chicago: Open Court Publishing Company, 1908.

———. *The Extra-Canonical Life of Christ: Being a Record of the Acts and Sayings of Jesus of Nazareth Drawn from Uninspired Sources*. New York: Funk & Wagnalls, 1903.

Pratscher, Wilhelm. *The Apostolic Fathers: An Introduction*. Waco, TX: Baylor University Press, 2010.

Resch, A. *Agrapha: Ausserkanonische Schriftfragmente*. 2nd ed. Texte und Unterschungen 30. Leipzig: Hinrichs, 1906.

Roberts, Alexander, James Donaldson, and A. Cleveland Coxe, eds. *The Apostolic Fathers with Justin Martyr and Irenaeus*. ANF 1. 10 vols. Buffalo, NY: Christian Literature Company, 1885.

Schoedel, William. *Ignatius of Antioch: A Commentary on the Letters of Ignatius of Antioch*. Edited by Helmut Koester. Hermeneia. Philadelphia: Fortress Press, 1985.

Scrivener, Frederick H., ed. *Bezae Codex Cantabrigiensis: Edited with A Critical Introduction, Annotations and Facsimiles.* Pittsburgh Reprint Series 5. Pittsburgh: Pickwick Press, 1978.

Stroker, William D. "Agrapha." *ABD* 1:92–95.

———. *Extracanonical Sayings of Jesus.* Society of Biblical Literature, 1989.

Trollope, W. S. *Justini Philosophi et Martyris cum Tryphone Judaeo Dialogus. Pars Prior, Colloquium Primi Diei Continens. Edited, with a Corrected Text and English Introductions and Notes.* Vol. 1. 2 vols. Cambridge: J. Hall, 1846.

Vielhauer, Philipp, and Georg Strecker. "IV. Jewish-Christian Gospels." Pages 134–78 in Vol. 1 of *New Testament Apocrypha.* Rev. ed. Edited by Wilhelm Schneemelcher. Translated by R. McL. Wilson. 2 vols. Louisville: Westminster John Knox, 1991.

Wright, Leon Edwin. *Alterations of the words of Jesus as quoted in the literature of the second century.* Harvard Historical Monographs 25. Oxford: Oxford University Press, 1952.

Yamauchi, E. M. "Agrapha." *ISBE* 1:69–71

———. "Logia." *ISBE* 3:152–54

INFANCY GOSPELS

Beyers, R., and J. Gijsel. *Libri de Nativitate Mariae: Psuedo-Matthae Evangelium, textus et commentarius.* CCSA 9. Turnhout: Brepols, 1997.

Bovon, François. "The Suspension of Time in Chapter 18 of Protevangelium Jacobi." Pages 393–405 in *The Future of Early Christianity: Essays in Honor of Helmut Koester.* Edited by B. Pearson. Minneapolis: Fortress, 1992.

Chartrand-Burke, Tony. "The Greek Manuscript Tradition of the Infancy Gospel of Thomas." Apocrypha 14 (2003): 129–51.

Cullmann, Oscar. "The Infancy Story of Thomas." Pages 439–52 in Vol. 1 of *New Testament Apocrypha.* Rev. ed. Edited by Wilhelm Schneemelcher. Translated by R. McL. Wilson. 2 vols. Louisville: Westminster John Knox, 1991.

———. "The Protevangelium of James." Pages 421–38 in Vol. 1 of *New Testament Apocrypha.* Rev. ed. Edited by Wilhelm Schneemelcher.

Translated by R. McL. Wilson. 2 vols. Louisville: Westminster John Knox, 1991.

———. "X. Infancy Gospels." Pages 414–69 in Vol. 1 of *New Testament Apocrypha*. Rev. ed. Edited by Wilhelm Schneemelcher. Translated by R. McL. Wilson. 2 vols. Louisville: Westminster John Knox, 1991.

Delatte, A. "Évangile de L'Enfance de Jacuies: Manuscrit No. 355 de la Bibliothèque Nationale." Pages 264–71 in Vol. 1 of *Anecdota Atheniensia*. Paris: Champion, 1927.

Frey, A. "Protévangile de Jacques." Pages 73–80 in Vol. 1 of Écrits apocryphes chrétiens. Edited by François Bovon and P. Geoltrain. Paris: Gallimard, 1997.

Gero, S. "The Infancy Gospel of Thomas: A Study of the Textual and Literary Problems." *Novum Testamentum* 13 (1971): 48–80.

Hock, R. F. *The Infancy Gospels of James and Thomas*. Santa Rosa, CA: Polebridge, 1995.

———. *The Life of Mary and Birth of Jesus: The Ancient Infancy Gospel of James*. Berkeley: Ulysses Press, 1997.

Mirecki, Paul Allan. "Thomas, The Infancy Gospel of." *ABD* 6:540–44.

Smid, H. R. *Protevangelium Jacobi: A Commentary*. Translated by G. E. van Baaren-Pape. Apocrypha Novi Testamenti I. Assen: Van Gorcum, 1965.

van Stempvoort, P. A. "The Protevangelium Jacobi, the Sources of its Theme and Style and their Bearing on its Date." Pages 410–26 in vol. 3 of *Studia Evangelica*. Edited by F. Cross. Berlin: Akademie Verlag, 1964.

Strycker, E. de. *La forme la plus ancienne du Protévangile de Jacques*. Brussels: Société des Bollandistes, 1961.

Testuz, M. *Papyrus Bodmer V: Nativité de Marie*. Geneva: Bibliotheca Bodmeriana, 1958.

Voicu, S. J. "Histoire de l'enfance de Jésus." Pages 191–96 in Vol. 1 of Écrits apocryphes chrétiens. Edited by François Bovon and P. Geoltrain. Paris: Gallimard, 1997.

———. "Notes sur l'histoire du texte de l'Histoire de l'enfance de Jésus." *Apocrypha* 2 (1991): 119–32.

Vorster, Willem S. "James, Protevangelium of." *ABD* 3:629–32.

PASSION GOSPELS

Allen, W. C. "The 'New Sayings of Jesus'." *The Guardian*. London, July 27, 1904.

Attridge, H. W. "The Greek Fragments." Pages 95–128 in *Nag Hammadi Codex II, 2–7 together with XII.2*, Brit Lib. Or 4926 (1) and P.Oxy 1, 654, 655*. Edited by B. Layton. Leiden: Brill, 1989.

Bouriant, U. *Fragments du texte grec du livre d'Enoch et de quelques écrits attribués à saint Pierre*. Mémoires publiés par les membres de la Mission archéologique française au Caire 9.1. Paris: Ernest Leroux, 1892.

Brown, R. E. "The Gospel of Peter and Canonical Gospel Priority." *New Testament Studies* 33 (1987): 321–43.

Coles, R. A. "2949. Fragments of an Apocryphal Gospel (?)." Pages 15–16 in Vol. 41 of *The Oxyrhynchus Papyri*. Edited by G. M. Browne, R. A. Coles, J. R. Rea, J. C. Shelton, and E. G. Turner. London: Egypt Exploration Society, 1972.

Crossan, J. D. *The Cross That Spoke: The Origins of the Passion Narrative*. San Francisco: Harper & Row, 1988.

Denker, J. *Die theologiegeschichtliche Stellng des Petrusevangeliums: Ein Beitrag zur Frügeschichte des Doketismus*. Bern-Frankfurt: M. Lang, 1975.

Evelyn-White, H. G. *The Sayings of Jesus from Oxyrhynchus*. Cambridge: Cambridge University Press, 1920.

Fitzmyer, J. A. *Essays on the Semitic Background of the New Testament*. London: Geoffrey Chapman, 1971.

———. "The Oxyrhynchus logoi of Jesus and the Coptic Gospel according to Thomas." *Theological Studies* 20 (1959): 505–60.

Foster, Paul. "Are There Any Early Fragments of the So-Called Gospel of Peter?" *New Testament Studies* 52 (2006): 1–28.

———. "P.Oxy. 2949—Its Transcription and Significance: A Response to Thomas Wayment." *Journal of Biblical Literature* 129 (2010): 173–76.

———. *The Gospel of Peter: Introduction, Critical Edition and Commentary*. Critical. Texts and Editions for New Testament Study. Leiden: Brill, 2010.

Gebhardt, O. von. *Das Evangelium und die Apokalypse des Petrus*. Leipzig: J. C. Hinrichs'sche Buchhandlung, 1893.

Goodacre, Mark. "A Walking, Talking Cross or the Walking, Talking Crucified One?" *NT Blog*, October 18, 2010. Online: http:// ntweblog.blogspot.com/2010/10/walking-talking-cross-or-walking.html.

Gounelle, R. "Évangile de Nicodème ou Actes de Pilate." Pages 249–59 in Vol. 2 of Écrits apocryphes chrétiens. Edited by P. Geoltrain and J.-D. Kaestli. Paris: Gallimard, 2005.

Green, J.B. "The Gospel of Peter: Source for a Pre-canonical Passion Narrative?" *Zeitschrift für die neutestamentliche Wissenschaft und die Kunde der älteren Kirche* 72 (1987): 216–22.

Grenfell, Bernard P., and Arthur S. Hunt. "1. ΛΟΓΙΑ ΙΗΣΟΥ." Pages 1–3 in Vol. 1 of *The Oxyrhynchus Papyri*. London: Egypt Exploration Fund, 1898.

———. "654. New Sayings of Jesus." Pages 1–22 in Vol. 4 of *The Oxyrhynchus Papyri*. London: Egypt Exploration Fund, 1904.

———. "655. Fragment of a Lost Gospel." Pages 22–28 in Vol. 4 of *The Oxyrhynchus Papyri*. London: Egypt Exploration Fund, 1904.

———. *New Sayings of Jesus and Fragment of a Lost Gospel from Oxyrhynchus*. London: Oxford University Press, 1904.

———. ΛΟΓΙΑ ΙΗΣΟΥ: *Sayings of Our Lord from an Early Greek Papyrus*. London: Henry Frowde, 1897.

Harnack, A. *Bruchstücke des Evangeliums und der Apokalypse des Petrus*. Leipzig: J. C. Hinrichs'sche Buchhandlung, 1893.

Hilgenfeld, A. "Neue gnostische Logia Jesu." *Zeitschrift für wissenschaftliche Theologie* 47 (1904): 567–73.

Hofius, O. "Das koptische Thomasevangelium und die Oxyrhynchus-Papyri Nr. 1, 654 und 655." *Evangelische Theologie* 20 (1960): 21–41, 182–92.

Hurtado, Larry. "The Greek Fragments of the Gospel of Thomas as Artefacts: Papyrological Observations on Papyrus Oxyrhynchus 1, Papyrus Oxrhynchus 654 and Papyrus Oxrhynchus 655." Pages 19–32 in *Das Thomasevangelium: Enstehung—Rezeption—Theologie*. Edited by Jorg Frey, Enno Edzard Popkes, and Jens Schroeter. Berlin: Walter de Gruyter, 2008.

Izydorczk, Z. *Manuscripts of the Evangelium Nicodemi: A Census*. Toronto: Pontifical Institute of Mediaeval Studies, 1993.

————. *The Medieval Gospel of Nicodemus: Texts, Intertexts, and Contexts in Western Europe*. Tempe, AZ: Medieval and Renaissance Texts and Studies, 1997.

Kasser, R. *L'Évangile selon Thomas: Présentation et commentaire théologique*. Neuchatel, Switzerland: Delachaux & Niestlé, 1961.

Kraft, R. A. "Oxyrhynchus Papyrus 655 Reconsidered." *Harvard Theological Review* 54 (1961): 253–62.

Kraus, Thomas J., and Tobias Nicklas. *Die Petrusevangelium und die Petrusapokalypse: Die griechischen Fragmente it deutscher und englischer Übersetzung*. Berlin: de Gruyter, 2004.

Lods, A. *Reproduction en héliogravure du manuscrit d'Enoch ed des écrits attribués à saint Pierre*. Mémoires publiés par les membres de la Mission archéologique française au Caire 9.3. Paris: Ernest Leroux, 1893.

Lührmann, D. "Kann es wirklich keine frühe Handschrift des Petrusevangeliums geben?" *Novum Testamentum* 48 (2006): 379–83.

————. "POx 2949: EvPt 3–5 in einer Handschrift des 2ten/3ten Jahrhunderts." *Zeitschrift für die neutestamentliche Wissenschaft und die Kunde der älteren Kirche* 72 (1981): 216–26.

Lührmann, D., and P. J. Parsons. "4009: Gospel of Peter?" Pages 1–5 in Vol. 60 of *The Oxyrhynchus Papyri*. Edited by R. A. Coles, M. W. Haslam, and P. J. Parsons. London: Egypt Exploration Fund, 1898.

Mara, M. G. *Evangile de Pierre*. Sources chrétiennes 201. Paris: Cerf, 1973.

McCant, J. W. "The Gospel of Peter: Docetism Reconsidered." *New Testament Studies* 30 (1984): 258–73.

Michelsen, J. H. A. "Nieuw-ontdekte fragmenten van evangeliën." Pages 153–64 in Vol. 3 of *Teyler's theologisch tijdschrift*. 1905.

Mirecki, Paul Allan. "Peter, Gospel of." *ABD* 5:279–81.

Robinson, J. A. "The Gospel according to Peter." *The Gospel according to Peter and the Revelation of Peter: Two Lectures on the Newly Recovered Fragments Together with the Greek Texts*. Edited by M. R. James and J. A. Robinson. London: C. J. Clay, 1892.

Scheidweiler, F. "The Gospel of Nicodemus / Acts of Pilate and Christ's Descent into Hell." Pages 501–5 in Vol. 1 of *New Testament*

Apocrypha. Edited by Wilhelm Schneemelcher. Translated by R. McL. Wilson. 2 vols. Louisville: Westminster John Knox, 1991.

Smith, Ben C. "The gospel of Peter." *TextExcavation*, n.d. http://www. textexcavation.com/gospelpeter.html.

Swete, H. B. *The Akhmîm Fragment of the Apocryphal Gospel of Peter*. London: Macmillan, 1893.

Vaganay, L. *L'Evangile de Pierre*. 2nd ed. Paris: Gabalda, 1930.

Wayment, Thomas A. "A Reexamination of the Text of P.Oxy. 2949." *Journal of Biblical Literature* 128 (2009): 375–82.

Zahn, T. *Das Evangelium des Petrus*. Erlangen: Deichert, 1893.

POST-RESURRECTION GOSPELS

John Rylands University Library. "Gospel of Mary - Rylands Papri - Greek Papyrus 463 - Recto." *John Rylands University Library Image Collections*, n.d.

———. "Gospel of Mary - Rylands Papri - Greek Papyrus 463 - Verso." *John Rylands University Library Image Collections*, n.d.

King, K. *The Gospel of Mary of Magdala: Jesus and the First Woman Apostle*. Santa Rosa, CA: Polebridge, 2003.

Lührmann, D. "Die griechischen Fragmente des ariaevangeliums Pox 3525 und Pryl 463." *Novum Testamentum* 30 (1988): 321–38.

Macquarie University. "Gospel of Mary." *XVI Excerpts from Apocryphal Books*, 2005. http://mq.edu.au/pubstatic/public/download/?id=45136

Morard, F. "Évangile selon Marie." Pages 5–13 in Vol. 2 of Écrits apocryphes chrétiens. Edited by P. Geoltrain and J.-D. Kaestli. Paris: Gallimard, 2005.

"P.Oxy.L 3525." *POxy: Oxyrhynchus Online*. http://www.papyrology.ox.ac. uk/POxy/

Parsons, P. J. "3525. Gospel of Mary." Pages 12–14 in Vol. 50 of *The Oxyrhynchus Papyri*. London: Egypt Exploration Society, 1983.

Pasquier, A., ed. *L'Évangile selon Marie*. 2nd ed. BG 1. Laval: Les Presses de l'Université Laval, 2007.

Perkins, Pheme. "Mary, Gospel of." *ABD* 4:583–84.

Puech, H.-C., and B. Blatz. "The Gospel of Mary." Pages 391–95 in Vol. 1 of *New Testament Apocrypha*. Rev. ed. Edited by Wilhelm

Schneemelcher. Translated by R. McL. Wilson. 2 vols. Louisville: Westminster John Knox, 1991.

Roberts, C. H. "463. The Gospel of Mary." Pages 18–23 in Vol. 3 of *Catalogue of the Greek and Latin Papyri in the John Rylands Library*. Manchester: University of Manchester Press, 1938.

Till, W. C., and H.-M. Schencke. *Die gnostischen Schriften des koptischen Papyrus Berolinensis 8502*. Rev. ed. Berlin: Akademie Verlag, 1972.

Tuckett, Christopher, ed. *The Gospel of Mary*. Oxford Early Christian Gospel Texts. Oxford: Oxford University Press, 2007.

FRAGMENTS

Bell, Sir Harold I., and T.C. Skeat. *The New Gospel Fragments*. London: Oxford University Press, 1935.

———, eds. *Fragments of an Unknown Gospel and Other Early Christian Papyri*. New impression. London: British Museum Press, 1935.

Bertrand, D. A. "Papyrus Egerton 2." Pages 37–42 in Vol. 1 of *Écrits apocryphes chrétiens*. Edited by François Bovon and P. Geoltrain. Paris: Gallimard, 1997.

———. "Papyrus Oxyrhynque 1224." Pages 417–18 in Vol. 1 of *Écrits apocryphes chrétiens*. Edited by François Bovon and P. Geoltrain. Paris: Gallimard, 1997.

Bickell, G. "Das nichtkanonische Evangelienfragment." Pages 53–61 in Vol. 1 of *Mittheilungen aus der Sammlung der Papyrus Erzherzog Rainer*. Edited by J. Karabacek. Vienna: Verlag der k.k. Hof und Staatsdruckerei, 1887.

———. "Ein Papyrusfragment eines nichtkanonischen Evangeliums." *Zeitschrift für katholische Theologie* 9 (1885): 498–504.

———. "Ein Papyrusfragment eines nichtkanonischen Evangeliums." *Zeitschrift für katholische Theologie* 10 (1886): 208–9.

Bonaccorsi, G., ed. *Vangeli apocryphi I*. Florence: Libreria Editrice Fiorentina, 1948.

Bovon, François. "Fragment Oxyrhynchus 840, Fragment of a Lost Gospel, Witness of an Early Christian Controversy over Purity." *Journal of Biblical Literature* 119 (2000): 705–28.

Chapa, J. "5072. Uncanonical Gospel?" Pages 1–19 in Vol. 76 of *The Oxyrhynchus Papyri*. Edited by J. Chapa and D. Colomo. London: Egypt Exploration Society, 2012.

———. "A newly published 'gospel fragment'." *Early Christianity* 3, no. 3 (September 2012): 381–89.

Charlesworth, James H., and Craig A. Evans. "Jesus in the Agrapha and Apocryphal Gospels." Pages 479–533 in *Studying the Historical Jesus: Evaluations of the State of Current Research*. Edited by Bruce D. Chilton and Craig A. Evans. New Testament Tools and Studies 19. Leiden: Brill, 1994.

Crossan, J. D. *Four Other Gospels: Shadows on the Contours of Canon*. New York: Harper & Row, 1985.

Deissmann, Adolf. *Light from the Ancient East: The New Testament Illustrated by Recently Discovered Texts of the Graeco-Roman World*. Translated by Lionel Richard Mortimer Strachan. London: Hodder & Stoughton, 1910.

Dodd, C. H. *A New Gospel*. Manchester: The Librarian, The John Rylands Library, 1936.

Foster, Paul. "Bold Claims, Wishful Thinking, and Lessons about Dating Manuscripts from Papyrus Egerton 2." Pages 193–211 in *The World of Jesus and the Early Church: Identity and Interpretation in Early Communities of Faith*. Edited by Craig A. Evans. Peabody, MA: Hendrickson, 2011.

Goodspeed, E. J., and I. A. Sparks. "Papyrus." *ISBE* 3:651–55.

Grenfell, Bernard P., and Arthur S. Hunt. "1224. Uncanonical Gospel." Pages 1–10 in Vol. 10 of *The Oxyrhynchus Papyri*. London: Egypt Exploration Fund, 1914.

———. *Fragment of an Uncanonical Gospel from Oxyrhynchus*. Oxford: Oxford, 1908.

Grenfell, Bernard P., and Arthur S. Hunt, eds. "210. Early Christian Fragment." Pages 9–10 in Vol. 2 of *The Oxyrhynchus Papyri*. London: Egypt Exploration Fund, 1899.

———. "840. Fragment of an Uncanonical Gospel." Pages 1–10 in Vol. 5 of *The Oxyrhynchus Papyri*. London: Egypt Exploration Fund, 1908.

———. *Catalogue Général des Antiquités Égyptiennes du Musée du Caire, Nos. 10001–10869: Greek Papyri*. Oxford: University Press, 1903.

Gronewald, Michael. "255. Unbekanntes Evangelium oder
Evangelienharmonie (Fragment aus dem Evangelium Egerton)."
Pages 136–45 in Vol. 6 of *Kölner Papyri*. Edited by Michael
Gronewald, B. Kramer, K. Maresch, M. Parca, and C. Römer.
Opladen: Westdeutscher Verlag, 1987.

Jeremias, J., and Wilhelm Schneemelcher. "Fragments of Unknown
Gospels." Pages 91–109 in vol. 1 of *New Testament Apocrypha*. Rev.
ed. Edited by Wilhelm Schneemelcher. Translated by R. McL.
Wilson. 2 vols. Louisville: Westminster John Knox, 1991.

Jeremias, Joachim, and Wilhelm Schneemelcher. "1. Oxyrhynchus
Papyrus 840." Pages 94–95 in vol. 1 of *New Testament Apocrypha*.
Rev. ed. Edited by Wilhelm Schneemelcher. Translated by R. McL.
Wilson. 2 vols. Louisville: Westminster John Knox, 1991.

———. "2. Papyrus Egerton 2." Pages 96–99 in vol. 1 of *New Testament
Apocrypha*. Rev. ed. Edited by Wilhelm Schneemelcher. Translated
by R. McL. Wilson. 2 vols. Louisville: Westminster John Knox,
1991.

Kannaday, Wayne C. *Apologetic Discourse and the Scribal Tradition:
Evidence of the Influence of Apologetic Interests on the Text of the
Canonical Gospels*. Text-Critical Studies. Atlanta: Society of
Biblical Literature, 2004.

Klostermann, E. *Apocrypha II: Evangelien*. 3d ed. Berlin: de Gruyter, 1929.

Koester, Helmut. *Ancient Christian Gospels: Their History and Development*.
Philadelphia: Trinity Press International, 1990.

Kraeling, Carl H. *A Greek Fragment of Tatian's Diatessaron from Dura:
Edited with Facsimile, Transcription, and Introduction*. Studies and
Documents 3. London: Christophers, 1935.

Kraus, Thomas J. "1. P.Vindob.G 2325: 'The Fayûm Fragment'." Pages
219–27 in *Gospel Fragments*. Edited by Thomas J. Kraus, Michael J.
Kruger, and Tobias Nicklas. Oxford Early Christian Gospel Texts.
Oxford: Oxford University Press, 2009.

———. "2. P.Berol 11710." Pages 228–39 in *Gospel Fragments*. Edited by
Thomas J. Kraus, Michael J. Kruger, and Tobias Nicklas. Oxford
Early Christian Gospel Texts. Oxford: Oxford University Press,
2009.

———. "3. P.Cair.G 10735." Pages 240–51 in *Gospel Fragments*. Edited by Thomas J. Kraus, Michael J. Kruger, and Tobias Nicklas. Oxford Early Christian Gospel Texts. Oxford: Oxford University Press, 2009.

———. "4. P.Mert. 51." Pages 252–63 in *Gospel Fragments*. Edited by Thomas J. Kraus, Michael J. Kruger, and Tobias Nicklas. Oxford Early Christian Gospel Texts. Oxford: Oxford University Press, 2009.

———. "5. P.Oxy. 1224." Pages 264–80 in *Gospel Fragments*. Edited by Thomas J. Kraus, Michael J. Kruger, and Tobias Nicklas. Oxford Early Christian Gospel Texts. Oxford: Oxford University Press, 2009.

Kraus, Thomas J., and Tobias Nicklas, eds. *Early Christian Manuscripts*. Texts and Editions for New Testament Study 5. Leiden: Brill, 2010.

Kraus, Thomas J. "P.Vindob.G 2325: Das sogenannte Fayûm-Evangelium— Neuedition und kritische Rückschlüsse." *Zeitschrift für Antikes Christentum* 5 (2001): 197–212.

———. "Reconstructing Fragmentary Manuscripts—Chances and Limitations." Pages 1–38 in *Early Christian Manuscripts*. Edited by Thomas J. Kraus and Tobias Nicklas. Texts and Editions for New Testament Study 5. Leiden: Brill, 2010.

Kruger, Michael J. "II. Papyrus Oxyrhynchus 840." Pages 123–215 in *Gospel Fragments*. Edited by Thomas J. Kraus, Michael J. Kruger, and Tobias Nicklas. Oxford Early Christan Gospel Texts. Oxford: Oxford University Press, 2009.

———. "P.Oxy. 840: Amulet or Miniature Codex?" *Journal of Theological Studies* 53 (2002): 81–94.

———. *The Gospel of the Savior: An Analysis of P.Oxy. 840 and Its Place in the Gospel Traditions of Early Christianity*. Leiden: Brill, 2005.

Lagrange, M. J. "Nouveau fragment non canonique relatif à l'Évangile." *Revue Biblique* 5 (1908): 538–53.

Landau, Brent and Stanley E. Porter, "Papyrus Oxyrhynchus 210: A New Translation and Introduction." Pages 109–124 in *New Testament Apocrypha: More Noncanonical Scriptures*. Edited by Tony Burke and Brent Landau. Grand Rapids: Wm. B. Eerdmans, 2016.

Lietzmann, H. "Ein apokryphes Evangelienfragment." *Zeitschrift für die neutestamentliche Wissenschaft und die Kunde der älteren Kirche* 22 (1923): 153–54.

Lührmann, D. "Das neue Fragment des PEgerton 2 (PKöln 255)." Pages 2239–55 in vol. 3 of *The Four Gospels*. Edited by F. Van Segbroeck. 3 vols. BETL 100. Leuven: Peeters, 1992.

Lührmann, D., and E. Schlarb. *Fragmente apokryph gewordener Evangelien in Griechischer und lateinischer Sprache.* Marburger theologische Studien 59. Marburg: N. G. Elwert, 2000.

Mayeda, G. *Das Leben-Jesu-Fragment: Paprus Egerton 2 und seine Stellung in der urchristlichen Literaturgeschichte.* Bern: Verlag Paul Haupt, 1946.

Moreschini, Claudio, and Enrico Norelli. "10. Fragmentary Gospels." Pages 64–68 in Vol. 1 of *Early Christian Greek And Latin Literature: A Literary History.* Translated by Matthew J. O'Connell. 2 vols. Peabody, MA: Hendrickson, 2005.

Neirynck, F. "Papyrus Egerton 2 and the Healing of the Leper." *Ephemerides Theologicae Lovanensis* 61 (1985): 153–60.

Nicklas, Tobias. "1. The 'Unknown Gospel' on Papyrus Egerton 2 (+ Papyrus Cologne 255)." Pages 11–120 in *Gospel Fragments*. Edited by Thomas J. Kraus, Michael J. Kruger, and Tobias Nicklas. Oxford Early Christian Gospel Texts. Oxford: Oxford University Press, 2009.

Nicklas, Tobias, Thomas J. Kraus, and Michael J. Kruger, eds. *Gospel Fragments*. Oxford Early Christian Gospel Texts. Oxford: Oxford University Press, 2009.

Parker, D. C., D. K. G. Taylor, and M. S. Goodacre. "The Dura-Europos Gospel Harmony." Pages 192–228 in *Studies in the Early Text of the Gospels and Acts: The Papers of the First Birmingham Colloquium on the Textual Criticism of the New Testament*. Edited by D. K. G. Taylor. Text-Critical Studies. Atlanta: Society of Biblical Literature, 1999.

Petersen, William L. *The Diatessaron: Its Creation, Dissemenation, Significance and History in Scholarship*. Leiden: Brill, 1994.

Ponder, Ross P., "Papyrus Oxyrhynchus 5072: A New Translation and Introduction." Pages 125–139 in *New Testament Apocrypha: More*

Noncanonical Scriptures. Edited by Tony Burke and Brent Landau. Grand Rapids: Wm. B. Eerdmans, 2016.

Porter, Stanley E. "Early Apocryphal Gospels and the New Testament Text." Pages 350–70 in *The Early Text of the New Testament*. Edited by Charles E. Hill and Michael J. Kruger. New York; Oxford: Oxford University Press, 2012.

———. "POxy II 210 as an Apocryphal Gospel and the Development of Egyptian Christianity." Pages 1095–1108 in vol. 2 of *Atti del XXII Congresso internazionale di papirologia: Firenze, 23–29 agosto 1998*. Edited by I. Andorlini, G. Bastianini, M. Manfredi, and G. Menci. Firenze: Istituto papirologico "G. Vitelli," 2001.

Rees, B. R. "51. Christian Fragment." Pages 1–4 in vol. 2 of *A Descriptive Catalogue of the Greek Papyri in the Collection of Wilfred Merton, F.S.A.* Edited by B. R. Rees, Sir Harold I. Bell, and J. W. B. Barns. 3 vols. Merton Papyri. Dublin: Hodges Figgis, 1959.

Roberts, C. H. "An Early Christian Papyrus." Pages 293–96 in *Miscellània papirològica Ramon Roca-Puig*. Edited by S. Janeras. Barcelona: Fundació Salvador Vives Casajuana, 1987.

Schneemelcher, Wilhelm. "3. Oxyrhynchus Papyrus 1224." Page 100 in vol. 1 of *New Testament Apocrypha*. Rev. ed. Edited by Wilhelm Schneemelcher. Translated by R. McL. Wilson. 2 vols. Louisville: Westminster John Knox, 1991.

———. "4. Papyrus Cairensis 10 735." Page 101 in vol. 1 of *New Testament Apocrypha*. Rev. ed. Edited by Wilhelm Schneemelcher. Translated by R. McL. Wilson. 2 vols. Louisville: Westminster John Knox, 1991.

———. "5. The so-called Fayyum Fragment." Page 102 in vol. 1 of *New Testament Apocrypha*. Rev. ed. Edited by Wilhelm Schneemelcher. Translated by R. McL. Wilson. 2 vols. Louisville: Westminster John Knox, 1991.

Schwartz, D. R. " 'Viewing the Holy Utensils' (P. Ox. V, 840)." *New Testament Studies* 32 (1986): 153–59.

Sparks, I. A. "Parchment." *ISBE* 3:663.

Swete, H. B. *Two New Gospel Fragments*. Cambridge: Deighton, Bell & Co., 1908.

Wessely, C. "Fragments de collections de prétendues sentences de Jésus." Pages 151–82 in *Les plus anciens monuments du christianisme écrits sur papyrus*. Patrologia Orientalis 4.2. Paris: Firmin-Didot, 1906.

———. "Textes Divers de la Littérature Chrétienne." Pages 490–95 in *Les plus anciens monuments du christianisme écrits sur papyrus II*. Patrologia Orientalis 18.3. Paris: Firmin-Didot, 1907.

Wright, D. F. "Apocryphal Gospels: The 'Unknown Gospel' (P. Egerton 2) and the Gospel of Peter." Pages 207–32 in *The Jesus Tradition Outside the Gospels*. Edited by D. Wenham. Gospel Perspectives 5. Sheffield: JSOT Press, 1985.